A WORKING
MOTHER'S
GPS

A WORKING MOTHER'S GPS

A Guide to Parenting Success for the Modern Working Mom

ATARA MALACH

LIFESTYLE
ENTREPRENEURS
PRESS
LAS VEGAS, NV

ISBN: 978-1-948787-08-6
Published by
Lifestyle Entrepreneurs Press
Las Vegas, NV

If you are interested in publishing through Lifestyle Entrepreneurs Press, write to: *Publishing@LifestyleEntrepreneursPress.com*

Publications or foreign rights acquisitions of our catalog books. Learn More: *www.LifestyleEntrepreneursPress.com*

Printed in the USA

In order to maintain anonymity of the mothers in my GPS groups, I have changed names and other identifying characteristics, such as occupations and children's names.

Guidelines to Parenting Success (GPS) Online Program

Lifetime access to Atara Malach's groundbreaking parenting program for working mothers!

You will be empowered to parent your children with confidence and love. These practical and proven GPS skills will transform your relationship with your children. You will find these skills equally beneficial in the workplace.

The Guidelines to Parenting Success Online Study Program contains powerful and effective parenting lessons delivered across 26 short practical trainings to increase your confidence as a working parent.

As a special Reader Bonus you'll also receive a mini-masterclass on work/life balance which you can access and revisit any time. From the initial Parenting Color Interactive Quiz to your completed and personalized Parenting Roadmap to the bonus reports for single and blended family working mothers, you'll have all the tools you need to be an amazing working mom.

With the GPS Online Study Program you'll have all the tools you need for *Greater* Parenting Success!

Get Started Now:

www.AtaraMalach.com/gps1

DEDICATION

Did you think this book would be dedicated to someone
you didn't know? Not this time.
This book is dedicated to all the devoted, overworked,
frustrated, valiant, determined, working mothers. Mothers
who love so much, they invest all they have in becoming
the best working mother possible.
I learned from you. I am inspired by you.
This one is for you.

As a special gift for you, my readers, please use the following link to access my Special Reader Bonus, a free gift to you.

https://www.ataramalach.com/special-reader-bonus/

TABLE OF CONTENTS

A WORKING MOTHER'S

GPS

INTRODUCTION

HOW IT ALL BEGAN

I remember the first driving lesson I ever had. I was sitting safely buckled in the driver's seat, both hands gripping the steering wheel, heart pounding, staring straight ahead. The driving instructor told me to turn the ignition on and press softly on the accelerator. I was aghast. Start driving right then, with absolutely no experience? I should put the car in drive and start moving? I had never driven a car before, so naturally I was horrified by the prospect of injuring an innocent pedestrian, or at the very least, crashing into a parked car. Was she kidding?

But that's how we all begin our journey, isn't it? Whether it's on the road as an inexperienced driver or the moment we hold our first child in our arms; at one point in time, we were all new at this. In the case of parenting, nobody taught us how to do it; we were pretty much told to press on the accelerator before we knew how to drive. This is the scary, yet awesome, journey we take as parents, learning along the way as we move through the highways of our lives. It is exhilarating, exhausting and the most rewarding accomplishment we can ever experience.

Nobody prepared me adequately for how hard it is to be a mother. But what I found most challenging was not realizing how difficult it would be to raise happy children

1

while pursuing my career. When my first child was born I was not only calm, but absolutely positive about my future. I had my life all planned out: I would love being a mother while continuing to devote as much time as necessary to thrive at work. What I didn't realize was how conflicted and torn I would feel every minute of every single day.

What about you? When you're at work do you feel you should be home with your sick child or new baby? When you're at home are you often preoccupied with your issues at work? Do you feel exhausted, overwhelmed, frustrated, and guilty while trying to raise your young children and give your all to your career? Are you tired of feeling that wherever you are you should be someplace else, or that no matter how hard you try, it's never enough?

If you answered yes to any of these questions, then this book is for you.

I struggled with these same feelings for many years while raising my children as I built my private practice. My goal was to make everyone happy, and when I couldn't do that, I tried even harder. I loved being a mother to my six beautiful children, but I also enjoyed every minute I spent with my clients. My work was meaningful and important to me and I didn't want to give up anything in either part of my life. I wondered, "Why, when I have a rewarding career and an amazing family am I feeling so overwhelmed, frustrated, and resentful most of the time?"

The truth is I loved doing certain things for my family. Baking for a school event. *Of course.* Sitting in the park with other mothers watching my children on the swings and slides. *How could I give that up?* Creating treasured family traditions and giving each child individual attention. *Wasn't that what good parenting was all about?*

But I also loved my job. Long hours in the library researching my thesis. *No problem.* Staying extra hours in my private practice to build a reputation as a caring and dedicated professional. *Wasn't that absolutely necessary?*

While my list of obligations was endless and the demands were ever growing, my patience was almost nonexistent. And I was tired. I was always *so* tired.

Then, one evening, everything changed.

I was invited to speak to a large audience of working mothers about how to become better mothers, wouldn't you know? I had prepared everything ahead of time so that I could leave my children fed, loved, and almost asleep—but that didn't happen. Despite my heroic efforts my youngest, then four, parked himself in front of the door and refused to let me leave.

Nothing I did or said calmed him or convinced him, and I had to gently but firmly remove him from his defiant stakeout so that I could walk out the door. My heart was breaking as tears filled my eyes.

On my way to the lecture I told myself, "This is not what I signed up for. This isn't what I'm supposed to be doing. I'm not happy helping working women become better mothers while my children are so upset. There has to be a better way. I don't want to do this anymore."

That was the moment I wondered if I could create a parenting system that would work better for me and for the thousands of other working mothers I had connected to and learned from over the years. Using my years of struggle as a working mother and dedicated therapist, I sought to create an effective parenting method for working mothers who felt the way I did.

I am assuming that your career, your business, and your profession is important to you. And it should be. You have likely invested a great deal of time, effort, and financial resources to get where you are professionally today. You may even have plans to obtain a promotion, earn a post-graduate degree, or open yet another branch of your business. Your work might be necessary for you to survive financially, or it may also be your life's dream—something that adds meaning to your days. In short, whatever your personal situation is, work is probably an integral part of your life.

I imagine that raising a family, being a mother, and seeing your children grow into wonderful human beings who contribute to society and emulate your life values is your life's mission. As is true for me, it makes everything you are and everything you do eminently worthwhile.

This dichotomy is our constant struggle. Our role as a mother is vital and of eternal value. Yet our professional endeavors limit the time we have for our children. This causes tremendous stress as well as constant guilt. You may be feeling torn, even tormented, as you juggle the demands of your work and the commitment to your home, your children, and your role as a mother.

This is why I set out to find a way to parent my children with less confusion and guilt, and to discover a system that would allow me to gain clarity and save time. In doing so, I created a set of guidelines that not only helped me, but can now help you create loving relationships with your children and allow you to enjoy raising them while still devoting time to your work.

Feeling skeptical?

What if I told you that you *already know* everything you need to know about how to parent with confidence and be the mother every child loves, despite the long hours you spend at work? What if all you had to do was apply the universally recognized road signs as guidelines and then implement them in your parenting journey based on your personal comfort level and each child's individual personality?

If this sounds too good to be true, I've got good news for you: It's truly that simple.

My Working Mother's GPS (A **G**uide to **P**arenting **S**uccess) is based on the universal rules of the road that you have recognized and followed ever since you first crossed a street or drove a car. You already know what to do and how; you're utilizing this valuable knowledge on a daily basis anytime you go somewhere. All you have to do to enhance your life as a mom is to apply this knowledge to your parenting and customize it to your unique personality and family situation.

The basic components in any successful parenting plan have a combination of the following necessary elements: authority, trust, and love. Your children constantly need to feel that you are the authority, that you know what you are doing, and that you take full responsibility. They also need to feel they can trust you, which helps them to gain confidence and learn to trust themselves. And, above all, children need to feel loved and treasured.

The Working Mother's GPS system is comprised of three specific elements: universal road symbols, parental empowerment, and flexibility.

First, it's based on the traffic light we all recognize:

➢ The Green light emphasizes loving communication and how to encourage and connect, which fosters a long-lasting, loving relationship with our children.

➢ The Red light is the symbol of authority, or when and how to say no, deal with conflict and encourage self-control.

➢ The Yellow light symbolizes caution, allowing us to learn how to trust ourselves as parents and how to maximize daily interactions so that we earn our children's trust.

Note here that I've put the colors in a slightly different linear order than how an actual traffic light is viewed. I have done this because beginning with authority and rules, before setting the foundation of love and positive communication, actually backfires, igniting frustration for both parent and child. The last thing we want is for overworked parents to create resentful children. This is why we begin with the Green light of love.

My system also uses road signs we are all familiar with, which means you won't have to learn an entirely new parenting language. For any time-challenged working mother, this is a fantastic bonus. Each traffic light section of the book features two coordinating road signs:

- Green =
  - Mile Marker (consistency and encouragement)
  - Park and Ride (creative solutions)
- Red =
  - All-Way Stop (dealing with conflict)
  - Do Not Enter (self-control)
- Yellow =
  - Slippery When Wet (slowing down)
  - Intersection Ahead (preparing for transitions)

Second, the program is geared to empower you to be the adult and the parent, while feeling comfortable and confident staying in the driver's seat, no matter how your children challenge you. This minimizes the frustration and guilt that is usually the result of responding to their childish behavior and expecting children to behave as adults.

And third, it is flexible because you have full control over how to adjust the components of love, authority, and trust according to your child's needs, the situation, or your own preference at that moment. This gives you complete command of how and when to use these guidelines, which ensures a smooth ride to wherever you and your children need to arrive.

Obviously when your partner is on board and supporting you on this amazing journey, you will feel more confident and focused when planning your parenting roadmap. But even if you have differing needs and expectations, this program will bring out the best in each of you and allow you to complement each other while jointly parenting your children.

Once you feel clear about these guidelines, that's when the magic begins!

You, as a devoted mother, are the biggest expert on who your child is: you know how sensitive he is or how stubborn she is, you realize when he needs boundaries or when she needs more confidence, you also know that parenting a toddler is very different from what you can expect of a twelve-year-old.

Because this system combines love, authority, and trust, you will be able to decide in every interaction with each of your children, at any age or stage, how many of these components you want to emphasize at any given moment. Because we're using common road signs as guideposts to successful parenting, there is the added advantage of the signs being recognized by our partners and children, so that cooperation and success are much more likely.

While this book is aimed at working women, you can also benefit if you are not a working mother. This unique system will add to your parenting skills and enhance your relationship with your children no matter your situation. And although I've chosen to use examples for children aged two through twelve throughout this book—because there are such varying levels of understanding during that age span—all of my techniques can be applied to teens as well.

But this proven, practical, and proactive system goes beyond parenting, which is another reason it is unique among the thousands of parenting books out there. The powerful skills and guidelines you'll discover in *A Working Mother's GPS* will not only transform your relationship with your children, but they will be equally effective in enhancing your relationships at work. This double benefit allows working mothers to implement the exact same skills in the workplace that they've mastered at home, thus assuring their success in their careers as well as with their children.

The best way to make the most of this book is to first read through the chapters once. Reading the book in its entirety will help you understand the traffic light parenting method, which is laid out in three parts—Green, Red, and Yellow—each consisting of the following:

- ➢ Using the traffic signal as a parental guiding light.
- ➢ Overcoming bumps in the road that can make change difficult.
- ➢ Applying speed tactics to create faster results.
- ➢ Utilizing pertinent road signs to boost your parenting proficiency.
- ➢ Frequently asked questions posed by other working mothers just like you.
- ➢ A "through the rearview mirror" motivational recap to put you firmly in the driver's seat.
- ➢ Implementing your new skills like a pro in the workplace.

As you understand the importance of each "traffic light" and discover new skills, you will feel empowered to parent your children with confidence and clarity, as well as augment your skills when implemented at work.

In all walks of life we encounter bumps in the road. Driving is a perfect example of this. As we drive down the roads and highways of life, we encounter bumps, potholes, construction delays, accidents, and so much more, all of which slows us down or causes us to change our route and directions. Just as in driving, parenting has its own unique set of bumps in the road. Throughout this guide you will find a section in each chapter about possible "bumps in the road." These sections will help you prepare for when you may need to change directions or rethink your route as a parent.

While driving down the road as a parent, just as in a car, we are going to encounter times when we need to regulate or adjust our speed. In a car the speedometer tells you how fast you are going and you can press the accelerator to speed up. As a parent you will find times you need to speed up by pressing the accelerator. These tactics will be referred to as "speed tactics." Throughout this guide you will find a section in each chapter about speed tactics you may wish to employ. These sections will help you prepare for when you need to speed up by using the skills you have gained.

Eva, a mother of four children ages two to twelve, who also manages an HR department in a large firm, shared the following:

> I was very skeptical about starting yet another parenting program. I am an avid reader and have read scores of parenting books. What that accomplished was to confuse me completely. Each expert had another opinion about dealing with children. I needed to memorize how to respond if my daughter didn't want to eat her vegetables, but then react in a totally different manner when she was speaking disrespectfully or refusing to share her toys. I kept running to my books

to find the specific pages that held the sage advice I needed at that moment. And when I needed to deal with a situation that wasn't described in the books, I was lost.

With "A Working Mother's GPS," once I grasped the components, I was able to utilize and implement them in every single situation, no matter what was happening! This saves so much time and minimizes confusion. I use the same skills for my toddler scattering toys as I do with my twelve-year-old not doing his homework. I feel competent and confident instead of confused and frustrated. And best of all I can implement most of these skills at work. It's beyond amazing.

Like many important things in life, parenting is an ongoing process. When you begin to apply these parenting methods you will begin to notice what you are unclear about or struggling with, at which point you will benefit by going back to that particular section in the book and spending more time focusing on that specific aspect. Some mothers have shared that they keep this book handy to reread often, because each time they do, they notice something that they hadn't internalized before.

It might also be necessary for you to focus more intently on any chapter that doesn't come naturally for you. For example, mothers who find it easy to assert their authority may find it helpful to spend more time in the chapters on trust and love. Mothers who naturally create loving, encouraging home environments and a strong sense of trust, may find it important to spend more time in the chapter on authority.

However you approach it, know that in this parenting program you are constantly in the driver's seat. How you read, learn, internalize, and implement the various skills is entirely up to you.

With this book in hand, you now have at your fingertips an effective, successful parenting program based on input from thousands of working mothers worldwide. I invite you to grab this opportunity to begin implementing the valuable skills you will learn in the following pages. Your work and home lives *can* exist joyfully side by side, and the perfect time to start down the road to achieving that harmony is now. So press on the accelerator and enjoy this life-changing journey toward becoming the working mother you've dreamed of being, and the one your children will admire and love.

PART I

GREEN = LOVE = GO

PARENTING WITH GREEN

Do you remember the moment you first became a mother and the fierce, overwhelming love that filled your entire being, enveloping you and your child in a magical cocoon? You probably felt protective, proud, lucky, and overwhelmed all at once; this tiny bundle of joy was yours to love and nurture forever and you vowed to that little human being you would do just that.

Yet why, when we all love to love, most especially our children, do so many children feel unloved? Why do scores of overwhelmed and under-appreciated mothers admit to feelings of frustration and exasperation more often than being infused with undying love? If we indeed love our children so absolutely and completely, why is it that most mothers and children don't constantly feel it?

Creating a strong foundation of love is what the Green traffic light signifies in our GPS program, and this is why, as I mentioned in the introduction, we begin with Green and not with Red. Because of the stress that juggling home and work naturally creates—despite the fact that love exists in abundance—we need the awareness, insight, and skills to be able to use positive communication to convey that love.

To illustrate that further, let's explore how the Green light works as a parental guiding light.

USING THE GREEN LIGHT AS A PARENTAL GUIDING LIGHT

When you're on the road and see the light turn green ahead, what do you think? What do you feel? If you're like most, you feel happy to be able to keep your foot on the accelerator and continue on the way to your destination. Of course, you need to constantly be aware of what is happening around you to make sure there is no danger to you, other vehicles, pedestrians, or passengers. For example, if you're a cautious driver, you might instinctively slow down when cruising through an intersection, but overall you feel energized and happy to be on your way.

Of all the symbols and road signs in this parenting system, this one might seem unnecessary to you at first glance, because every mother knows how to love her child, right? But have you actually given enough thought to that statement? Is it always so easy to love?

Each of us wants our children to feel the love we have for them. But a hectic life with responsibilities at home and at work, very little time, and our need to handle a wide array of discipline issues can camouflage this love to seem more like frustration than adoration. So what can we do to overcome these challenges and reignite the love we have for each of our children?

15

My answer lies in a question: What would it take for you to fall in love with your child? Yes, you read that correctly! Fall in love with your child. And not only love her (I know you do), but fall *in love* with her?

Remember what falling in love feels like? If not, let me remind you.

When you're in love you feel that you're the luckiest person to have met that special someone. You spend day and night focusing on all the positive qualities they may have (despite anything to the contrary that those around you are trying to point out) and come up with creative ideas to show them how you feel. You invest time in thinking up ways to surprise them or do something thoughtful to make their heart sing. You consistently take joy in the similarities between you; convincing yourself they are your soul mate. You are highly aware of their likes and dislikes and accommodate them on any and all issues without complaint. I can go on and on, but I won't.

So the question is, when was the last time you felt this way about your children?

When you look at them do you see the sparkle in their eyes and notice the charming dimple, or are you too busy focusing on the untucked shirt or the missing button? When you scan their report card does your heart swell with pride at the strides they have taken, or are your eyes quickly scrolling down the grades, comparing them to those of last year, or to those earned by another child, and instead feel disappointed and upset?

I want to be clear that when you love your children it doesn't prevent you from emphasizing things you think they should and could do better, all for their benefit, of course. But when you are *in love* with your child, there is a powerful positive force that fills you both with energy and hope. This doesn't mean you won't have to parent them or teach them about life's countless rules. When you see your children as unique and special, they will feel the much-needed confidence your parental support conveys and they can flourish beyond expectations. So how can you fall in love with your child?

Before giving some practical suggestions, I am reminded of something that happened to me in the early 1980's. I was a mother of three young children, living in cramped quarters in a small apartment on the first floor. There was no place for any of us to move around. If the children wanted to play, the baby would invariably wake up. For meals we had to eat in shifts in our tiny kitchen.

After a while we decided to sell this apartment and look for something bigger and more accommodating for our family. The brokers told me to prepare a newspaper advertisement. As I was writing the advertisement, describing the advantages of our small home that would entice prospective buyers, I began to realize that there were numerous positive aspects of our living conditions that I had completely overlooked. It was in a beautiful neighborhood with young families who had children the exact ages of mine. There was a park behind the building and the front yard was lush with budding shrubbery, beautiful flowers, and benches where we moms could sit and chat while the children romped and played far away from dangerous traffic. It was also close to shopping, schools and doctors' offices, yet had the feel of the suburbs. For those of us who didn't have a car at our disposal, it was also conveniently close to public transportation.

Several people called, excited to have a chance at living in such a wonderful place. In fact I had a multitude of serious buyers who were willing to overlook the cramped quarters because of all these advantages. And guess what? We decided not to sell it after all. Instead we stayed in that apartment for another ten years, enjoying every moment we spent there.

Do you know what changed for me after being so unhappy there for so long? Once I was forced to describe the multiple advantages of our home, I was able to fall in love with it again, appreciate the many benefits, and learn to ignore its few drawbacks. In other words, when I was compelled to focus on the apartment's positive features for inclusion in the advertisement, my entire attitude changed. After experiencing that amazing turnaround I used the same method to fall in love with my children.

THREE CREATIVE WAYS TO FALL IN LOVE WITH YOUR CHILD

Create a picture album for each of your children

Creating an album is a sure-fire way to connect you to the special feelings you had the moment your child was born. You can create a scrapbook-type album letting your creativity have free rein or a digital album with video clips, which makes it really come alive.

I suggest beginning with your child's birth, your stay in the hospital, and their tiny footprints. Add baby memorabilia and anything else you collected through the years. Allow yourself to go back to when they first came into your life and invest time in creating a loving tribute to each child.

As you work on this album, connect to the hopes, dreams, and excitement you had during the first few months you became acquainted. Capture the tremendous love you felt during those life-changing moments and hold on to those feelings for as long as you can. Also, share with your child what you are creating and let them join in the fun. Together you can create happy memories while compiling as many pictures and as much content as you can gather.

To add a further dimension to your trip down memory lane, conduct an interview with your child and record it on video or audio. You will find that spending time involved and invested in connecting to the pure, powerful love you felt from the moment each child was born will reignite any dormant feelings that have been covered by layers of frustration and obligations.

I'm confident that once you embark on the process, you'll find yourself falling in love all over again!

Create a personal advertisement for your child

No, your child is not an apartment and he or she is definitely *not* for sale! This is an exercise that when done seriously is usually an invaluable eye-opener. Using your imagination start writing and see what you come up with.

The following is an example of an ad a mother shared with one of the GPS groups I have led.

> *Maggie is an adorable eight-year-old girl who loves the color lilac. She has a great sense of humor and loves making babies smile. She has learned to put her stuff back where it belongs and says thank you to old ladies who give her candy, if I remind her quickly enough. She loves to cuddle in bed with me on cold winter mornings and can sing any song she has heard only once. She brings me my slippers when she sees me kick off my stilettos after work and she shares her candy with her younger brother, despite the fact that he constantly annoys her.*

I have no doubt that an ad extolling the virtues of your child could continue for several pages. At the same time, I imagine you could conjure up some not-so-pleasant traits about your child, such as that she hates going to sleep, argues with you about who got the bigger slice of pizza, and never brings home important notes from her teacher. But, when you focus solely on her positive traits and charming characteristics, do you find that your heart quickens when you realize she is *your* daughter?

Try it and see what happens. If at first you don't succeed, give it some time and come back to it. Or ask for help from doting grandparents, extended family, and friends who know her. Notice how much there is to love.

Get to know your child

Here is where you get to explore what your child enjoys. Does he like to drink water or juice? Does she like to dance or read? If he had ten dollars what would he spend it on? If she had an hour with you, what would she likely choose to do? Who is his best friend? Or worst enemy? What is her best subject at school and what did she cry about last?

Hopefully you know the answers to these questions. But if I asked you more in-depth questions about your children, are you confident that your responses would be on target? Questions such as: What does he hate most about the fact that you work? What does she take most pride in pertaining to your job? What would he hide from you? What has she shared with you that nobody else knows?

When we are in love with someone we have a constant thirst to know and learn more about them. Each piece of information makes us feel closer and more connected. Yes, you gave birth to your daughter. Yes, you feed, clothe, and support your son, but you will be surprised to learn how much you *don't* know about your child. You will be even more surprised to learn how getting to know your child—taking a true interest in what they do, say, think, want, hope, and are afraid of—can strengthen the love you have for them.

"To know me is to love me," is an oft-repeated truism, but it certainly applies to us as parents. With that in mind, "date" your children; get to know them. When you do, you'll see how easy it is for you to feel more connected and loving than you may have felt in a long time.

After you have practiced the above-mentioned suggestions and have seen and felt your love grow and enhance your relationship, it will be much easier to implement the important skills associated with the Green road symbols.

Let's start learning how to express appreciation and love by first examining how our children interpret what we say and how we say it.

WHAT YOUR CHILD HEARS: STOP OR GO?

If you recorded all your interactions with your children from morning till night, what would you notice? Might it be that although you love your children, what they *hear* when you're nervous or what they interpret when you're too busy, usually contradicts this enduring love? Said another way, do our words give the impression that we're pressing on the accelerator or slamming on the brakes?

It would be wonderful if our children could plumb the depths of our hearts and feel the love we have for them. But since they haven't experienced this indescribable parent–child bond, they can only judge by what they hear and see, not by what we may be feeling, no matter how intense and eternal that love is.

When a child *feels* your love and has consistent *proof* that you love them, they are empowered by this reality to better face the world; as if you've enabled their internal accelerator. They feel equipped to weather life's challenges while learning to love themselves, love life, and love those around them.

But in order for that to happen, they need to hear and see you express those positive emotions consistently.

Terri, a mother of four and an interior designer with a busy private practice, said:

> *Since I was a little girl playing with dolls all I ever wished for was to be a mother. I used to daydream about the darling children I would have and the fun things we would do together. I imagined afternoon tea parties and walks in the park and ice cream on hot summer days. But for some reason that never happened. I have children, but am not really having fun or feeling loving. I find myself rushing through my days angry and frustrated. I can't figure out who I'm angry with more, myself or them. This is NOT what I signed up for.*

Have you ever felt this way? Have you come home after a long day at work and snapped at your children and then wondered who you've become? Do you cringe when you realize that everything you promised yourself you wouldn't say or do is exactly what your children hear and experience day after day?

This is the great paradox most working mothers contend with—the brake you unwittingly slam on without even realizing it—that is wrapped up in the powerful impact that our words, and how we say them, have on our relationships.

In our Working Mother's GPS program, one of the ways the Green traffic light symbolizes "go" is in giving the wondrous energy of love and engaging in loving communication. Words not only paint pictures of our emotions, but they lend weight and give meaning to the myriad gestures we extend to our children and loved ones. Being aware of their enormous influence allows us to learn how to harness their power.

FOSTERING
STRONG BONDS

Though we may consistently juggle hectic schedules and suffer from lack of sleep, we can never lose awareness of how powerful our words are and what far-reaching effects they have on our children. What you say and how you say it will shape your relationship with your child forever; which is why this topic deserves our full attention.

Think about it: the only way people know what we're thinking, or what we want and need, is by what we say, how we say it, and how we act before, during, and after we speak. As we progress through this book we're going to explore envisioning the red and yellow traffic lights for specific reasons, but for now I want you to practice imagining a green light in your mind as you communicate; reminding you that Green symbolizes love. Once this becomes a habit, then what you convey—even in times when you must be assertive or when you may be angry or frustrated—will be aligned with communicating love through your words. When you do this as a parent, your children will consistently receive a solid foundation of self-esteem and a loving connection upon which to build their future, no matter what the situation or emotions involved. In other words, infusing your words with love fills their emotional fuel tank.

While you may think expressing love to your child is something you regularly do, think about the following questions and reflect honestly on your answers.

> ➢ What does your child hear you say to him or her in the morning while you are rushing to work and school?
> ➢ What do they hear you say in the evening while they are doing their homework or during bedtime?

As you consider these questions thoughtfully, can you hear your tone of voice? Can you feel the emotions behind your words? Are you perhaps cringing as you realize what they usually hear?

While its totally understandable that the words and tone you've been using are typically uttered after being up in the wee hours with your child, a full stressful day at work, or exhausted after rushing around to their numerous activities; it's important that you understand that words said indiscriminately are often painful and many times, indelible.

Does the following sound familiar?

Isabelle! Get in here this minute! How many times do I have to tell you to take your plate to the sink before you leave the table? And what is your school bag doing on the dining room floor? Can't you EVER put ANYTHING in its place?

Liam, I was very disappointed by what I heard at the PTA last night. Do you know how much I've spent on tutors for you during the last three months? That money was supposed to go for the new car we need. Imagine how I felt when I heard that you aren't even using this investment the way you should be. Despite all this tutoring, you received failing grades in three subjects! What do you have to say for yourself?

Put yourself in these children's shoes and try to imagine what they think or feel when bombarded by such talk. Do you think if asked they would answer that they felt loved?

In the above two examples, irate and overwhelmed working mothers are clearly expressing their displeasure and making their children feel attacked, criticized, and as though they are the cause of their mother's frustration.

Here is how the rest of both exchanges may have gone.

Isabelle might have immediately defended herself by silently screaming that her mother never notices when she *does* take her plate to the sink and put her school bag where it belongs, which might be true. Or she might rightfully feel that if her mom's boss would call at that moment she would surely sound calm and interested. But when it comes to her daughter, she doesn't have the patience or the inclination to be calm and loving.

Liam might assume that it doesn't pay for him to try understanding any of his schoolwork anymore, especially after having sacrificed riding his bike with his friends after school for months because of all the tutoring. He *has* tried his best, which obviously isn't enough. If after all that effort, nothing's working out, and his teacher and mother are still hugely disappointed in him, why study anymore? If Liam thinks his mother will never be satisfied no matter how hard he tries, he might even come to an extreme conclusion: that he was born to be a loser.

When we express hurtful words to our children that convey criticism, shaming, labeling, comparisons, or sarcasm, the universal result is that your child will think negative thoughts about *themselves* ... and about *you*! Their thoughts may sound like, "I'm no good," or "My mother hates me."

As you consider the usual interactions between you and your children during the course of the day, are you surprised? Did you realize that despite being a devoted and loving mother (I *know* you are!), your children are hearing something else entirely? And most importantly, did you consider what they are telling themselves when they hear you express yourself this way?

If you had hoped they would think . . .

My mother loves me so much.

Or

Everything she's saying (screaming) is only for my good and because she's stressed for time.

Or

The entire reason she's working is because it's good for our family.

Or

> *How can I make things easier for her? I know she doesn't really mean what she's saying right now.*

How realistic do you think you are being? If your boss said similar things to you, how would you feel? Consider how you would feel if your boss said:

> *How many times do I have to tell you to format your reports with double spacing? Don't you remember anything at all? Do you ever think of anyone other than yourself?*

Or

> *I don't want to hear another word you have to say until you finish . . .*

Or

> *Don't you realize how much pressure I am under? Why would you make it worse by not proofreading the campaign?*

Perhaps your boss has legitimate reasons for being annoyed, but would you really feel validated, understood, and eager to redo your work if she said things like this to you on a daily basis? Of course not. If this is how your boss interacted with you most of the time, you might seriously consider complaining to HR about this behavior, or hand in your resignation.

Let's honestly examine what children usually tell themselves when subjected to constant pressure, criticism, and sarcasm.

> *I can never do anything right.*
> *Mom is never happy with me.*
> *I'm no good.*
> *She doesn't really love me.*
> *She's always angry with me.*
> *Better to stay out of her way so that she doesn't find something else to complain about.*

I know for a fact that this is *not* what you want your child to feel. Certainly this is the opposite result you envisioned when considering the devotion and loving care you consistently invest in your family, despite numerous work obligations.

So, what is the solution? How can we use the life-changing power of words to forge the bonds of love between ourselves and our children?

It can often be as simple as saying a loving hello, goodbye or thank you.

TWO IMPORTANT WORDS YOU MAY FORGET TO SAY

In today's highly pressurized society, we are all extremely busy. Not only do we work many hours of the day out of the house, but we are also overworked and overwhelmed by the never-ending responsibilities we have raising our children. Many of us also provide help to our extended families, as well as carving out time to contribute to our communities. This leaves little time for our social lives and ourselves—and even less time to notice the good in those around us.

Taking the time to simply say, "Hi" or "Goodbye," is one of the best investments you can make in your relationship with your children (or anyone else you care about).

You don't have to stop what you're doing; whether it's cooking dinner, folding laundry, or supervising other children. Simply make a point of personally greeting your child when he or she wakes up, comes home, walks into the kitchen in the morning, or returns from doing an errand or outdoor chore. Adding an endearment or their nickname is even better—every child loves to hear terms like "Hi, Sweetie" when he walks into a room, or "Bye, Janeykins" as she leaves for a friend's house.

It might seem like a small point, but the minute you begin to invest in consistently using this daily act of recognition and love, you will see that your child's reaction will be ample reward. Try it—you'll be amazed at what this verbal acknowledgment of their presence can create.

Think about it: your child is out of the house most of the day. Whether it's the younger ones in preschool or the older ones in grade school, they need to contend with—and maybe even compete with—many other children. In addition, they are expected to succeed scholastically as well as socially, and by the time they come home it is safe to guess that they are tired, hungry, and possibly out of sorts.

When your children clamber into the car after school, lessons, or sports, be sure to smile, make eye contact, and warmly greet them. If you're greeting your children when you get home from work, be sure to let your eyes light up when you see them and offer sincere affection. You'll notice that they are instantly energized and validated by your genuine, loving attention. When you are too busy to notice or acknowledge your children, they will feel ignored, unimportant, and unloved. This might be far from the truth, but it is their perception.

Think about how you feel when you're waiting for a store clerk to notice you or hoping a receptionist will finally look your way. You feel slighted or frustrated, right? So why then at home—in the place where our loved ones are supposed to feel the safest and most beloved—would we want our children to experience the opposite?

When we make it a point to greet our children by offering a simple, smile-filled, "Hi," we are saying, "I see you. I'm glad you're here. You're more important to me than anything else I'm doing at this moment." When your child is leaving the house to go to school or some other activity, walking him to the door and saying goodbye while wishing him well sends him off with words of love that will stay with him wherever he is going. This is the power of speech—and it is the magic of seeing the green traffic light in your mind's eye when you communicate. With one well-timed word we can create and strengthen a loving relationship.

Don't be surprised if this one small gesture leads to your child speaking to you, and his siblings, with more love and affection. By being a role model he can emulate, you are setting the stage for him to do the same.

CULTIVATING AN ATMOSPHERE OF GRATITUDE

Now that you have mastered the skill of using words to create tremendous results, you can move on to learning how to cultivate an atmosphere of gratitude in your family. Before you can express a positive emotion you first have to feel it, despite the times we may justifiably feel frustrated and upset. The Green light we envision when expressing love is also a great symbol for gratitude, which is connected to love. Sometimes we may feel challenged during hectic days when we are valiantly trying to do everything and make everyone happy, so try to imagine the Green light when you teach the valuable lesson of appreciation.

As parents, we can be inspiring role models for our children if we show them by our words and actions how to be happy and grateful for what they have. How many of us have witnessed our children being jealous when they compare their situation to others; wanting what their siblings have or acting miserable when they see those around them with more toys, better clothes, driving nicer cars, living in larger homes, or taking more exciting vacations? You've likely heard one or more versions of these statements at one time or another:

All my friends have a lot of shoes. I only have two pairs.
I feel like such a geek.

Why do our cousins have pools in their backyards? Why are we the only ones who are different?

Why can't we go to Florida in the winter or Switzerland in the summer? Most of my friends do. We're the only ones who always stay home!

Sure, you can begin explaining, arguing, negotiating, or even screaming. But what will any of that accomplish?

When you hear comments like this from your children, it's a fantastic moment to visualize the Green light, teach a life lesson, and share your attitude of gratitude by connecting to what they shared and then telling them what you think and feel.

Two pairs of shoes might seem too few to you and I understand how you might feel that way [you are connecting to their feelings], *but many children don't even have two pairs. You can choose to buy another pair with your birthday money—and since your birthday is coming up soon, it's definitely a choice you may want to consider.*

I too would love to have our own pool [you are expressing agreement]. *As soon as our budget covers the basics we can begin compiling a list of what extras we can afford. From the look on your face, I imagine a pool will be your top priority!*

It is wonderful to be able to go to nice places for vacations [you are connecting to their feelings], *but if we can't afford to travel we can always find ways to have fun and be happy while staying within our budget. Let's brainstorm some ideas!*

Using this Green GPS skill might not make your child stop wanting, comparing, or complaining, but when you accept and reflect back the importance of what they are saying and then add your adult outlook on the issue, you will be helping them view the situation from a different perspective. What this does is set the foundation for a healthy philosophy in life; having you as their compass— their personal role model.

Children aren't born knowing how to be satisfied and happy with what they have—they need to be taught. Therefore, if you make it a point to be happy with your lot in life, and verbalize your gratitude, it will be that much easier for your children to begin to internalize the same healthy, mature outlook. Be encouraged knowing the hundreds of times throughout your children's lives that you took the time to teach them important life lessons, you were influencing them to grow into responsible, realistic adults. Teaching them gratitude is not only making sure they are grateful for the many things they have, but also how to say thank you and express their gratitude to others—including you.

You deserve to be appreciated for the countless things you do, arrange, and initiate for your family and loved ones. You also deserve to be lauded for the time, effort, and creativity you invest in your profession. But the reality is that although you deserve appreciation and recognition, you might wait for weeks, months, or even years until you are commended, if at all, especially by your children.

Sure, we are not meant to be dependent on our children's words of appreciation, but imagine how much more aware and willing they may be to offer words of thanks when you set the example.

I remember when personally expressing appreciation with a beautiful card, and making the effort to mail it after someone extended kindness, was the norm. Whether it was for a gift received, a dinner party invitation, or a lovely weekend spent with friends, a personal thank-you note was the least that was expected. Nowadays, we're lucky to receive thanks in the form of an email or text.

While I'm not here to bemoan the decline of social niceties, I do wish to convey that we as parents set the standard of what constitutes good manners—and that includes expressions of gratitude. Think of the impact on your child when learning from you to respond to kindnesses and generosity with loving words; imagine sitting down together and teaching the value of a handwritten note. For us overburdened and unappreciated working mothers, taking this initiative to restore the lost art of gratitude is undeniably admirable; I offer heartfelt thanks to any mother who makes the effort to do this.

But don't just let me be the one to thank you. You may be pleasantly surprised one day soon to see your child take the initiative and write a thank-you card to someone. Although it isn't the primary goal, one of those lovely expressions of gratitude, penned in your child's own hand, may be written expressly to you.

OFFERING EFFECTIVE - NOT DEFECTIVE - COMPLIMENTS

Once you are used to expressing gratitude to your children for even the slightest positive actions, you will want to move on to acquiring the next Green skill: offering an effective compliment.

Contrary to popular belief, compliments aren't always easy to formulate or convey. What's more, as puzzling as it may seem, many people feel uncomfortable when they receive a compliment. Let's explore this for a moment. Who wouldn't want to hear nice things said to them or about them? It seems strange, right? There are actually several reasons why people are uncomfortable with compliments.

> ➢ They feel they don't truly deserve the glowing description that's offered.
> ➢ They feel compelled, sometimes awkwardly, to immediately return the compliment.
> ➢ They feel pressure if they believe they have to live up to the unrealistic expectations the compliment carries.
> ➢ They might believe the compliment is given solely to manipulate them into agreeing to do something they don't really want to do.

Being aware of some of the problems well-intentioned compliments can cause, you might wonder how a well-meaning compliment can result in so many mixed feelings. How can you confidently tell your children the positive things you think and feel about them without some of these complicated reactions?

The answer lies in the following secret: effective compliments don't refer to the person (*You are the best daughter!*) and they don't describe the end result (*Your homework is the neatest!*). When you give a compliment that focuses on *them* instead of on what you see and feel, most times they will resist or deny it.

For example, if you compliment your son or daughter by saying that they are good, obedient, smart, or wonderful, they may easily remember the times you felt the opposite and respond by thinking or saying, "No, I'm not. You're just saying that. You don't really mean it."

In contrast, an effective compliment that creates positive feelings is described by what you *see*, what you *feel*, and how that might *affect* you. It is not an opinion about *them* which they can easily refute.

Let's better understand this method of complimenting by using real-life examples of what works and what doesn't.

> *You are the best!* [A general statement that is easily doubted] *You behaved like a doll while I was working today.* [A vague interpretation of an end result]

Giving this "compliment" to your child could make her think:

> *I'm not the best! I ate three bags of candy Mom doesn't know about and all she cares about is if I let her work.*

Not exactly the intention you had when formulating that compliment, right? A more effective compliment would be:

> *When you played quietly so you didn't disturb me when I was busy working* [describing what you **saw**] *it made me feel so happy* [describing what you **feel**].

After hearing this, your child might say to herself:

> *Even though Mom was busy, she noticed how hard I tried to be quiet. And I love it when she's happy! I really am a great kid!*

I'm sure you will agree the statement above sounds much better. This type of effectively conveyed compliment accomplishes a few things. It proves that you paid attention to the details, it describes positive feelings you have for your child, and it usually results in your children complimenting themselves.

If you're concerned that constructing an effective compliment on the spot requires too much thought and is therefore difficult, let me assuage your concern right now. All it takes to create an effective compliment is to 1) describe a specific situation and 2) express how that makes you feel. By following this simple Green GPS template, you won't have to try hard to invent fictitious compliments. For example, you won't say, "You are so sweet," when truthfully you are thinking the exact opposite. In short, this is not about affixing a sticker of "wonderful" on your child's forehead; which is merely labeling, not complimenting.

When we compliment our children we are pointing out behaviors we notice they are doing or not doing. By connecting those behaviors to our feelings of gratitude we are taking this one step further.

Here is the template for your Green GPS arsenal that you can use over and over again:

When I [**see**, notice, realize, imagine, etc.] you doing/being_____, I **feel** _____ [proud, happy, calm, excited, etc.] and [how this **affects** you] _____.

Using this template you can see that instead of tossing out a general compliment, which can sound insincere and is usually less effective, you could say to your daughter:

*When I **see** how you do your homework on your own every evening even though you'd rather play with your friends, I **feel** happy and proud of you. The extra time that gives me allows me to prepare the lunches for tomorrow.* [How this **affects** you]

NOTICING UNINTENTIONAL POSITIVE BEHAVIOR

If at times you feel a bit challenged giving effective compliments when things are going smoothly, you probably think it's next to impossible to compliment your child when you're experiencing negative feelings toward him. However, if despite feeling frustrated, disappointed or hurt, you are still determined to find something positive about your child to comment on, there's a solution! You might choose to focus on *unintentional* positive behavior.

For example, your child is sitting quietly because she is tired. She's not *intentionally* doing anything "good," but she is giving you an *unintentional* gift of silence or cooperation. In such situations, you could say:

> *I noticed in the last ten minutes you didn't once interrupt your brother while he built a Lego tower* (although that was definitely not her intention) *and that made me so happy.*

Or your child might be engrossed in a book or game and you were able to take advantage of the relative quiet to make a call.

> *Keisha, you didn't bother me once during my long call to Grandma. I'm so proud of you being considerate!*

Keisha didn't intentionally mean to be considerate, but in calling out her unintentional behavior, you are maximizing a learning opportunity and giving her a positive outlook on herself. Try this Green GPS method of noticing your child doing something unintentionally positive, even when she has no idea she was doing it! You might be surprised by how effective this can be.

I have heard from many mothers who, after making it a point to begin using this highly effective Green GPS skill, admitted that consistent, positive communication and effectively constructed compliments often build a bridge of connection and cooperation—even when they thought their child was too resistant and hostile to be receptive.

Compliments that are genuine, specific and said in a loving manner are especially effective in difficult situations. Regardless of what happened before or what transpires afterward, when you take the opportunity to describe what you see, express what you feel, and speak in a loving manner, you'll enjoy the life-changing results.

One word of caution: When things aren't going well between you and your child, don't expect a response of gratitude or affection when you offer a compliment. Don't get discouraged and refrain from complimenting just because they're in a bad mood or going through a difficult phase. Seek out as many opportunities as possible to compliment effectively and know that positive results are occurring behind the scenes. For example: When you tell sullen Leah, "I noticed that you helped your sister put on her jacket before she went out. That was very thoughtful of you and I felt lucky to be your mom." Or you say to aggressive Aiden, "I saw you playing gently with the baby. That was very responsible and it made me feel happy and calm to see."

They may roll their eyes or they may say nothing in return. But they will listen. When you tell her she is a thoughtful daughter, when you express to him that he is a responsible older brother, they will begin to realize that you were describing reality as you saw it. Over time they will start to internalize your love and hopefully allow themselves the warm, wonderful feelings that genuine compliments are meant to create. Likewise, by using the Green GPS template, nobody can refute what you saw and what you felt, so it cannot be countered with a denial. You'll find that when you use this Green GPS skill often and with consistent passion, it is guaranteed to pay off. It will also go a long way in creating a lasting, loving bond between you and your child.

CATCHING YOUR CHILD DOING SOMETHING GOOD

We've discussed that to express the ever-growing love we have for our children we must communicate positive messages that reflect our true feelings for them. A fun way to do this is to try to catch your child doing something good— however big or small—as if you're playing a game or are on a treasure hunt.

I get it, we are so stressed for time, we tend to take good behavior for granted. When things are going smoothly we send up a silent prayer hoping it will continue. But when something upsets or disappoints us, we seem to have no trouble finding time to point it out.

> *Why are you speaking with your mouth full?*
> *Why is your light on way after bedtime?*
> *Why do you always complain when I ask you to do something?*

But ask yourself this: Does your son sometimes speak when his mouth *isn't* full? Does your daughter sometimes turn off her light when she's supposed to? Does either one surprise you at times by cooperating with you without resisting or negotiating?

If you answered yes to any of these questions (and I hope you did), then make it a point to notice, acknowledge, and express appreciation when you catch them doing what you asked of them.

> *I noticed during dinner you were being careful not to speak with your mouth full. I'm so proud of you!*
>
> *I saw your light was off by 8:30 pm last night. I really appreciate that.*
>
> *You said "Okay" the first time I asked you to pick up the toys. Thank you!*

Doesn't it feel great when you read these comments? I know . . . it might not be what you're used to doing, but if you assess the amount of time it takes to point out something negative, you'll realize that in that same amount of time you can express something positive. So use those few precious moments to enhance and improve your most important relationships.

When I practice this skill with mothers in the GPS groups they tell me they love this exercise and have a lot of fun with it. They find when they focus on "catching" their children doing something good, magical things happen.

Mary, a mother of four, owns a flower shop and works long hours. She describes herself as perpetually exhausted, frustrated, and feeling guilty about being away from home so many hours. This is what she shared with the GPS group after applying this piece of the Green skill set with her children.

> At first it was difficult for me to catch them doing anything good. I was so used to calling them out on the slightest infraction that I really had to train myself to **see** the good. But once I got used to it, I noticed something unexpected. My children began realizing and appreciating the good **I** was doing! They pointed out the times I read to them at night or had patience to play a board game with them. It's been beyond amazing!

What is obvious and encouraging from this feedback is that not only does the relationship between mother and child improve when using this positive green communication, but it has far-reaching, powerful "side-effects": children begin to express appreciation to their parents and to each other—and everyone gets to be part of the fun.

BUMPS IN THE ROAD

OVERLOOKING THE IMPORTANCE OF GRATITUDE

If I had to guess why we as parents overlook the importance of expressing gratitude toward our children, I would say it might be because we do so much at home and at work and hardly ever hear a thank you. As a result, we may subconsciously come to believe that it is unnecessary to make a big deal over a child brushing their teeth or when—after twenty reminders—they put their plate in the dishwasher. After all, we don't ask much of them, so they *should* be doing these tasks. Then why make a fuss and thank them? Isn't the little they do completely expected in return for all that we do for them? Yes . . . and no.

A home is not a hotel and each family member has specific responsibilities. Just like you don't get a thank you for making sure there is always fresh food and clean clothes no matter what your work schedule is, they shouldn't expect a thank you every time they fulfill any of their obligations. There's certain logic to that line of thinking. But it's also true that when something sounds logical, it is not always wise.

The reality is that we are usually more polite and thankful to strangers than we are to those we love most. In fact, we often treat our nearest and dearest with the least respect and appreciation, as if what they do and how they help is simply expected, or worse, too inconsequential for us to comment on. Yet we don't give a second thought to profusely thanking a stranger for holding the door for us.

It is here that I want to remind you that we set the standard. If we want our children to appreciate their many blessings in any form, we must be the role models. This means we have to be willing to express our appreciation for even the tiniest of things, because that's what cultivates an attitude of gratitude as a foundation of their lives—both inside and outside of the home.

I agree that when a mother consistently devotes night and day to taking care of her family and her home despite constant work pressures, she should be applauded and commended. I also believe that when children cooperate and behave graciously with siblings or guests it should be pointed out and celebrated. In short, human goodness should never be taken for granted. This is why I recommend that we as parents find every opportunity we can to share our positive feelings with our children, and a vital part of that is expressing gratitude and appreciation.

UNDERESTIMATING THE POWER OF TONE

Like everything else, the importance of a caring, affectionate tone can be overlooked when we are harried and multitasking. Obviously, the positive effect an affectionate comment will have is reduced dramatically when the words are said in an impatient or disinterested manner. Connect to your loving feelings and make sure your tone conveys warmth when telling your children how their behavior has made you happy/proud/grateful to be their mom. This way they will not only hear what you are saying, but they will be able to feel it and believe it. It's imperative that tone of voice be a primary focus: it's what gives the underlying meaning to the words we choose to say. If your children don't hear sincerity in your voice, or you speak in an impatient or disinterested manner, your "positive" comments will be reduced dramatically. The next time you formulate a compliment or want to share a loving feeling with your child, take an extra moment to be mindful of your tone of voice while conveying that all-powerful dose of verbal love. You will be glad that you did!

SPEED TACTICS

APPRECIATE WHAT THEY DON'T DO

An atmosphere of love and affection is created when those around you hear that you appreciate who they are and what they are doing. But there's a twist to this habit that also has positive effects: thanking somebody for what they *didn't* do. Sometimes it is more important to thank somebody for what they didn't do, because many times what someone didn't do goes unnoticed more often than what they did do.

Take a look at the following examples:

> *When you realized we had leftovers for dinner (again!) because I'm in the middle of a big project at work, you didn't complain. I really appreciate that!*

> *When I said I couldn't help you study for your civics test, you didn't argue. Instead, you called a friend and studied over the phone. I was really proud and appreciated you doing that.*

It's true that what *doesn't* occur tends to go unnoticed more often than what does, but when you utilize your Green = Love = Go skills to point out something you appreciate that your child *didn't* do or say, the circle of gratitude continues to grow.

BEGIN TODAY

Parents tend to do two things that stall their efforts in regard to gratitude; wait until they think they have these new skills down perfectly before they start trying them or wait until their children start being more grateful. Despite possibly not feeling ready, do start trying to implement these GPS skills now. No matter how under-appreciated you may feel as a mother, try to remain positive and focused. I know that can be tough, but when you make it a point to show gratitude, your children will begin to emulate you. What's more, by not starting now, you will most certainly miss out on thousands of opportunities in the coming years to say thank you to your children. We learn not to respond or react to childish behavior, but rather to demonstrate adult behavior and remain in the driver's seat at all times.

I encourage you to rise above your usual stress level and be a role model for your children—starting today. This is your opportunity to show all the appreciation you feel, despite the fact that you likely don't receive enough of the gratitude that you so clearly deserve. Once this Green GPS skill becomes a constant part of your verbal interactions, you may be surprised to find that your children follow your lead and begin appreciating you as well.

GREEN ROAD SIGNS TO BOOST YOUR PARENTING PROFICIENCY

Before we embark on our first road sign I want to reassure you that as parents it's a process learning to recognize and implement the messages of the road signs and their symbolic meanings. Here are a few things to keep in mind as you adopt these new practices.

At first you will be adjusting to which sign to use when. If the right sign doesn't come to you immediately, you might find yourself realizing all the ways you could have prevented the situation *after* it took place. That's okay. It's normal to need some time to calm down and think clearly. Sometimes, it may even be days later that it clicks which road sign would have been the biggest help to you. Rest assured that this is part of the process, but the more you practice the less you'll have to think about which sign is most applicable for the given situation.

Also, as you continue to internalize the messages of the various signs, you will begin to notice your behavior and interactions *during* the altercation—meaning that you've reached a heightened level of awareness. In other words, even though you're already in the midst of the situation, you might find yourself thinking about a better solution than the one you may be headed toward. It may feel a bit disconcerting to be embroiled in an exchange without a clear, chosen sign to steer it in the right direction, but it actually indicates progress; your mind is considering a desired solution, not merely being stuck in the heat of the moment.

In time, as a result of you investing your time and effort into utilizing this GPS skill set, you'll recognize and respond to the warning signs *before* a situation escalates beyond repair. This is a long-awaited indication that these empowering GPS skills have become an integral part of your parenting. Before you know it, you'll be so accustomed to visualizing the appropriate sign that the choice becomes almost automatic—allowing you to prevent or at least minimize most disputes before they happen.

GREEN MILE MARKER = CONSISTENCY AND ENCOURAGEMENT

This will be our first road sign on your journey to becoming a better working mom. Throughout the book, in each section, we will use road signs to symbolize certain skills for that section. Just as in the stoplight colors, the road signs will be familiar since you have seen them on the road as you travel day to day. Hopefully you will find the use of familiar road signs makes it easier to remember the associated actions with that sign. This first sign is the Green Mile Marker.

It lets us know that we're making progress toward our desired destination. It also provides a comforting self-check, even when everything is going as planned. The same is true for us as parents as we guide our children toward adulthood and more autonomy—and our families toward harmony. Because both consistency and encouragement are inherent in these goals and because they are vital components when raising our children as working mothers, it's the perfect sign to visualize when either of these topics is called into question.

Let's take a look at two circumstances with regard to consistency, which are symbolized by the Green Mile Marker.

CONSISTENCY

Every working mother understands when things are going smoothly it makes sense to keep our foot on the accelerator and continue doing whatever it is that's working. Yet reality has proven that despite creating dependable interactions and routines with our children, it isn't always easy to "stay in our lane." Why is this? Borrowing from the road analogy, while we may be cruising along just fine, we sometimes switch lanes to get where we're going faster or to distance ourselves from an annoying truck or car. Likewise when we're in a rush or we want to avoid certain outcomes, we abandon tried-and-true methods and often leave consistency behind.

To illustrate an example of this, Meredith, a mother of four and the founder of a national chain of health spas, shared the following:

> *I love my work and I'm a very hands-on mother. In order to create some kind of balance between work and home, I had the morning and evening routines down to a science. But I'm always looking for new ways to improve both at home and in my profession, so I joined the GPS group. When I learned about this Green Mile Marker, I was a bit impatient because I felt it was unnecessary. Little did I realize that I was in the midst of creating a crisis because I underestimated the importance of sticking to what had worked in the past. During the months I was expanding my business, I hurried my evening routine and cut out the private bedside conversations and bedtime stories. I also*

stopped writing funny Post-It notes to put into their lunch boxes every morning. Because I felt things were going well, I didn't think twice about cutting corners. In fact, when things came crashing down at home I didn't realize this was in response to my not being there for them in ways they had come to rely on. Now that we're back to our consistent routines, things have calmed down and I have a new respect for the importance of consistency, especially when things are going well.

We all have a tendency to let things go when we feel confident about our success. But that is precisely when we need the extra reminder about the importance of staying the course and validating and reinforcing what is going well.

CREATING ROUTINES AND TRADITIONS

Another way to remain consistent in your parenting journey is by recognizing the important roles that routines and traditions play in our busy lives. Here is where you can equate the mile marker sign to driving on cruise control. Consider your seemingly mundane routines or cherished traditions as a consistent path toward family joy and harmony, similar to traveling an open road that requires minimal concentration on the part of the driver.

Let's start with routines. Perhaps as you simply try to get through each day you haven't thought much about the fact that when lacking routine rules in your family, you will likely experience unending chaos. If this rings true for you, it's time to put some routines into place.

Here are two examples:

> *Laura, an accountant with three children, knew she needed to create a streamlined evening routine to get everyone to bed on time without going ballistic. After brainstorming a new nightly routine with her kids, they chose a song they all loved and decided to play it on high volume for five minutes to see if they could be ready for bed before the song ended. It was such a hit that she no longer had to fight with her kids to brush their teeth and get their pajamas on—a clear win for her!*

> *Sharon, a mother of seven-year-old twins, established a routine of Sunday night dinners for her family to sit down, discuss their week, talk, and laugh together. Even when there is basketball practice and homework due, she makes sure the Sunday night dinner tradition is sacred and never skipped.*

If you already have routines in place that are working for you, great! And if you have some that might need a bit of attention or tweaking, this may be the time to focus on those. Here's what Sarah, a mother of three and a popular photographer, experienced when she replaced her usual disarray with routines:

> *I'm a very laid-back mom and always took pride in my flexibility. When we discussed the importance of routines in the group I yawned and zoned out. A few months later, when I heard from one of the teachers*

at a PTA meeting that my son showed signs of difficulty adhering to any rules and regulations, I realized I was raising my children with no predictable order or routine. Up until then I felt if everyone was happy, it didn't matter what we did or when we did it. I now realize this is not only unrealistic, it is counterproductive for my children to be raised in such a haphazard manner. Since I have instituted routines in the mornings, evenings, and even on the weekends, my son has calmed down considerably and is doing much better in school. I am not ashamed to admit that I find my morning rush and bedtime hours much more efficient and enjoyable. And as an added bonus, I never imagined that learning how to better parent my children would not only enhance my skills as a mother, but also improve my professional standing with my clients.

Likewise, traditions create anchors for your family and are usually the fun aspect of creating consistency; the sky is the limit when it comes to holidays, birthdays, graduations, anniversaries or a personal family tradition. There is truly no end to what you can create traditions around, and each one creates a mile marker that everyone can look forward to reaching.

ENCOURAGEMENT

Now that we have discussed two critical aspects of consistency in parenting, (how to establish routines to create stability and streamline rush hours, and how to follow our routines, schedules and traditions despite pressure or distractions) let's examine two important methods for offering encouragement. Our mile marker is the perfect symbol to visualize both of the following skills.

OFFERING THAT EXTRA PUSH
IN THE RIGHT DIRECTION

When do you encourage your children? When things are going well for them or when they are discouraged? Probably both, right? Children (and mothers) need encouragement not only when they are aware of their accomplishments, but also when they are feeling down about their progress. As such, we use the subtle message of the Green Mile Marker—the one that reminds us how far we have come since starting out on our road trip—to symbolize the importance of ongoing encouragement and feedback. When we're reminded how far we have come, it gives us the extra push to continue on and reach our destination, or rather, to continue reaching for our goals. But we also need to be aware of giving a push in the right—not the wrong—direction.

Here are a few scenarios that may seem like no-brainers but are nonetheless great examples of expressing appreciation when your child does something well:

Your child plays softball and got her first hit. You say:

That was great how you kept your eye on the ball! The more you do that, the more hits you're likely to get!

Your son is getting along with your partner's children who join your family on alternate weekends. You say:

> *DeShawn, it was really amazing how you shared your room and made Jared and Malik feel so welcome here! Thanks to you, they look forward to spending time with us.*

Your daughter is watching your toddler in the park so you can finish up an important report for work. You say:

> *Emma, this is the third time you took Corey to the park so I could work without distractions. He comes back so happy! It's exciting to see how capable you are!*

When you express appreciation for your children's efforts during the times they do something well, they will find it easier to continue investing their energies, even if the taste of success causes them to want to slack off a bit.

Here are a few scenarios of what to say when your child is discouraged.

> *Harris, even though you weren't chosen for the starting lineup this time, you know how much you've been practicing and how you've improved your game. Your dedication and commitment are impressive!*

> *Quinn, I know you planned on serving this chocolate cake tonight for Grandma's birthday, but for a first-time baker I wouldn't worry at all that it's a little*

lopsided. We can decorate it with icing if you don't like the way it looks. What do you say?

I know you were hoping to get an A on that book report after you invested so many hours writing it, but this was great practice on how to write a book report, so next time it should be a breeze for you!

If you are consistent in acknowledging your children when they're feeling down about something that didn't go the way they hoped, your belief in them and focusing on what *was* done—and what still can be done—will jump-start their confidence and keep them in the fast lane.

USING SCAFFOLDING PRAISE AS
A SUPPORT TECHNIQUE

Some goals have a clear end result that may require a lot of time and effort to accomplish. When this is your child's situation—and her efforts haven't paid off yet—it is the perfect opportunity to use scaffolding praise. This is praise that isn't reserved for the final outcome, but instead encourages your children as they make their way toward their destination while on the road to success. Think of it this way: If the purpose of a scaffold is to support a building as it's being constructed or renovated, you can likewise think of praise as scaffolding supporting our children in the midst of a process, even if the final goal won't be reached in the foreseeable future.

The reason this is so important is because when we wait to praise our children when they have finally reached their goal, we are leaving them on their own during the long, and possibly lonely, road to their desired outcome. But when we envision the mile marker sign as a reminder to acknowledge and mark their progress along the way, we show them we are aware of their effort and appreciate them staying the course.

This type of praise might sound like:

> *I see how much effort you're putting into studying for your tests and doing extra credit to bring your grades up. I've noticed this semester you've devoted at least an hour each night to being on top of your schoolwork. I'm really proud of your perseverance.*

> *I know your goal is to be able to do fifty push-ups, but being able to do twenty-five right now is great! I know you've been trying to add a few more each week and look how far you've come since you started. Then you were only able to do ten!*

> *I noticed how you make it your priority to respond immediately to every friend who leaves you a message. I also overheard how nicely you treated the neighbors who came to play yesterday. That shows consideration and caring. Whoever has you for a friend is really lucky.*

Remember what the children reported feeling after their mothers praised them? Do you see how by using scaffolding praise the reaction would probably be much different? I would guess the child hearing his mother's comment about his grades might think that he is pretty great for being so serious about his school work and might even apply himself more consistently after being acknowledged for his effort. I am also betting that the daughter who heard how her mother noticed her efforts to be forthcoming and considerate with her friends would gain confidence in her social skills, instead of feeling frustrated that her mother labeled her popular, without really knowing what she had to contend with.

Can you see how these kinds of comments encourage children to continually apply themselves toward reaching a bigger goal? The mother talking about her son's push-ups is an obvious one with a clear goal that takes time to reach, but even a goal such as being more considerate or social, which requires incremental steps, can benefit from scaffolding praise. In any situation, if a child is consistently acknowledged for their effort, they're much more likely to not give up, even if they meet some challenges along the way. The next time you notice your child attempting to achieve a goal, or being consistent although they haven't yet accomplished their heart's desire, find something encouraging to say about where they are now. When you act as their vocal Green Mile Marker, you'll notice how they light up in response to your scaffolding praise—and how your words encourage them to continue on the road to their desired destination.

BUMPS IN THE ROAD

OFFERING UNREALISTIC ENCOURAGEMENT

Just like offering compliments that are *defective* instead of *effective*, there are pitfalls inherent in praising and encouraging our children the wrong way. When this happens children tend to feel pressured or confused, despite the well-meaning words of their parents. Here are two observations from children I've worked with:

> My mom always says she's sure I'll ace every subject. She thinks she's encouraging me, but she's really putting tons of pressure on me. School isn't fun because I'm afraid I'll let her down.

> When my mother assures me I'll be the most popular in my class, I just stare at her and think that she has no idea what my classmates are like. It's so ridiculous. My mother is supposed to know who I am. How can she be so clueless?

I have no doubt both of these mothers meant well, but you can see that their words of "encouragement," despite their good intentions, only served to create negative results. You can avoid making the same mistake by being aware of the pitfalls of offering exaggerated or thoughtless comments to your children disguised as encouragement.

OVERLOOKING THE "GOOD" CHILD

We usually invest a lot of energy in finding ways to connect to a child who is going through a rough time or making things difficult for us, right? But in tending to what we often call the "squeaky wheel" we often overlook the "good child," the one who behaves at home and in school and doesn't demand too much from us. I call these children "invisible;" because they do what is expected of them, don't actively ask for much attention, and thus they remain largely invisible.

While it probably goes without saying that "good" children are just as in need of our love and attention as their challenging siblings, it is nonetheless easy for us to miss the abundant opportunities we have to encourage and enjoy them. But when we envision the mile marker to remind ourselves of the importance of noticing and appreciating every child, we ensure that none of our children end up being ignored.

Marianne, a pharmacist and mother of two, shared the following:

I enjoyed everything we learned in the GPS groups. I even became a parenting guru to my friends and neighbors. But if I had to point to the most powerful takeaway from all the group meetings, it was this one vital point about noticing the invisible good children. I hadn't realized how much energy I had poured into my son who was a challenge from the moment he was born. He was the reason I signed up for this parenting program. What I didn't expect was to discover that my daughter was usually in his shadow. Because she consistently did well, I was able to essentially ignore her. When I realized this, I immediately made a U-turn and began to designate specific times to be alone with her. You wouldn't believe the difference that made. From being a shy, polite, passive child, she blossomed into an outgoing, happy, and affectionate daughter. I shudder to think I might have missed this and lost out on creating such a wonderful transformation.

SPEED TACTICS

MAKE YOUR CHILD FEEL NEEDED

Have you ever thought about the fact that most children today feel like they are a nuisance at best or a burden at worst? We do so much for them and with them...it's not like it was years ago when children were counted on to be an important part of the labor force at home and in the fields. Then, at a young age, children would collect the eggs, milk the cow or help tend the vegetable garden. They felt needed, important and knew their contribution was necessary and appreciated. Today children are mostly on the receiving end of things. We give and buy for them, drive them places and pay for their summer camps. Many times when their schedules stress us out, they realize the great financial burden they impose and feel frustrated, and sometimes even apologetic. When we show them what they can do and how we appreciate them, it adds to the cooperation and smooth functioning of the household. It raises self-esteem because your child will then be able to tell themselves, "Mom really needs me." For example, to your toddler you could say:

I really need your help to put away the toys so we can wake up to a clean house tomorrow.

To your eight-year-old you could say:

I need you to set the table for me before Grandma comes so I can do the cooking.

An eleven-year-old can be put "in charge" of looking after the pets of the household. The key component of this is to describe what you need and how you are relying on them to fulfill that task. For example, "Wow I couldn't have done it without you!" Or, "You make our dinnertimes run so smoothly!" By making them feel needed you're creating connection, cooperation and confidence!

CELEBRATE YOUR WINS

If you recognize and give yourself credit for investing in your journey toward successful parenting, you deserve a standing ovation. I know it's not easy raising your children with devotion and dedication while advancing in your career. If you don't celebrate yourself on a regular basis, I invite you to take a moment to notice the recent wins you have had with your children. Applaud the numerous parenting skills you have integrated and implemented since you began studying this book or joined our online program. By acknowledging the value of your dual roles and validating your progress as a working mother, you will not only be giving yourself much-deserved recognition, but you will also be modeling important behavior for your children to emulate.

Helen, a busy mother of three who has a thriving online business, shared this with the mothers in the group:

I have very high expectations of myself and those around me. This has served me well and has catapulted me to succeeding in almost every area of my life. But during discussion of this road sign, I realized I not only don't adequately applaud my progress as a mother, but I actually minimize the many positive changes I've made recently. Upon further contemplation, I noticed that I do the same with my children. This really shocked and saddened me. I saw myself as a very encouraging mom, but now I realize that I treat them as I treat myself, demanding nothing less than perfection.

Since I've become more validating and encouraging of myself, I see that it has already influenced my attitude toward my children's behavior. It's all very new to me, but I'm beginning to enjoy celebrating our small wins. It is my fervent hope that it isn't too late for my children to internalize this very powerful and positive mindset.

It's *my* fervent hope that going forward, you will practice and enjoy celebrating your wins—and that your children will join in applauding you as well.

GREEN PARK AND RIDE = CREATIVE SOLUTIONS

The Park and Ride road sign is the other sign in our Green GPS skill set because it conveys that although you might be comfortable in your vehicle at that moment, at times the easier, more efficient way to get to your destination might be to park your car and take a bus or train. How does this relate to parenting? The Park and Ride sign offers a creative solution for those who don't live near public transportation or for those who might want to use their car for part of their commute. It gives us, as parents, a mental reminder that creative solutions exist for the common problems we encounter while trying to raise happy children; at the same time still investing time and energy in our careers.

If using creativity to assess problems and respond to your children isn't your strong suit, I have good news: after working with thousands of mothers, I've identified three go-to ways you can use to solve just about any issue you're confronted with. When you abruptly arrive at a "station" you didn't anticipate, simply visualize the Park and Ride sign, thus giving you three alternative options for getting to your desired destination (problem solved). All you need to do is choose the vehicle (creative solution) that makes sense in your particular situation.

THREE CREATIVE PROBLEM-SOLVING VEHICLES

The first step to solving your problems in a creative way is learning how to properly identify challenges. Let's face it, not all problems are easy to solve, not all problems deserve equal attention, and some disappear without too much effort on our part when only a small, albeit important, change is made.

With that in mind, read through the following situations. What you glean from these scenarios will enhance your ability to reframe problems and solutions and your ability to do it with creativity, both at home and in the workplace.

Creative Vehicle #1

Recognize that the problem belongs to the person whose needs and desires are not being met.

Let's look at how Saraj, mother of Raj and full-time architect, dealt with the following situation:

THE PROBLEM

> *Raj was very upset one weekend and nothing we did seemed to make him happy. After a bit of prodding he told me that he was one of a few boys who hadn't been invited to a birthday party taking place that day for one of his classmates. He felt rejected and angry, and wasn't in the mood to do anything pleasurable or productive that day.*

Do you view this as a problem? Of course, you do. As a parent, you can surely empathize with a child who's been left out. But what's important to recognize is that while it's a problem, it's not *your* problem. Raj being upset because he feels left out is *his* problem since *his* needs to be included and enjoy the party with the rest of his classmates aren't being met. What does this mean for you as a parent?

Once you assume ownership over someone else's problem, whether at work or at home, it actually does become a problem you have to deal with. In addition, you then take on the problem as a reflection of you, as Saraj does here:

> *Why weren't you invited to Jacob's party? I've done everything to help you learn how to be a good friend, so this doesn't make sense. I'm out of ideas for you kid. . . . I don't know what else I can do at this point.*

What Saraj does here is a common scenario. Caring, devoted mothers become over-involved in their children's lives because they have their children's best interests in mind. But when we as mothers act as if the problem and frustration is *ours*, it pushes our child's feelings aside, makes it all about us and prevents our child from being proactive in dealing with their problem.

In this case, Saraj needed to remove herself from the equation and focus on helping Raj cope with *his* disappointment, not hers.

THE SOLUTION

"Raj, I can imagine how upsetting it is to be home today when most of your friends are at Jacob's party (empathetic response reflecting his feelings without introducing her disappointment at his lack of social standing). *It seems as though some kids don't invite the entire class to their birthday parties* (teaching him to normalize this occurrence and have a healthier, less personal response to this fact). *When we plan your birthday party next month, we will invite all your classmates so no one will feel the way you do now. Meanwhile, you can let me know if you think of something you want to do today that will make you feel better.*

By realizing who the problem really belonged to (Raj, not his mother) Saraj was able to remain calm and connected while allowing Raj to express his feelings. At the same time she encouraged him to respond in a mature manner by combining her Green GPS skills of loving communication and creative problem solving. Here, instead of making Raj's problem hers, Saraj shows empathy for the emotions he's experiencing and offers a few questions to prompt Raj to deal with the disappointment on his own. The next time you face a problem stop and ask yourself, "Is this truly my problem, or am I making it mine when in reality it "belongs" to someone else? You might be happily surprised by the answer and even more thrilled to see what your children are capable of if you allow them to come up with their own creative solutions.

Creative Vehicle #2

Attempt to identify a single cause for a cluster of problems.

Imagine you're a harried mom with a long list of frustrations (this may not be a stretch for you to imagine). Think about how you would approach this scenario before reading the solution.

THE PROBLEM

Everything's been feeling off. Lately you've been sending your children off to school in a rush, nervous about arriving late to work. When you get home your baby clings to you from the moment you walk in the door until you put her to sleep. In addition, you come home to a messy house with piles of laundry so the few minutes you used to have to yourself are spent doing housework that's usually done by the housekeeper. Your partner also recently snapped at you because you've been running out of household staples more often than usual. All of this causes you tremendous stress which makes your days at work, as well as your time at home, exhausting and frustrating. Not to mention the cold silence between you and your partner that's weighing heavily on your heart. In short, no one is happy and you feel it all falls on you to fix.

This is certainly a daunting list of frustrations. But, if you take a few minutes to list these problems and analyze them, you might discover a common source.

THE SOLUTION

In this situation we'll call this mother, Kate. When Kate writes down all the things that are creating chaos within her family, she sees a pattern; most or all of these issues are related to the fact that her new housekeeper/babysitter—we'll call her Emily—is really not a good fit. Here are the reasons she uncovers during her brainstorm:

➤ Because Emily is not punctual, Kate is under pressure every morning to finish getting the kids ready for school, which invariably causes her to arrive to work late.
➤ Because Emily hasn't yet connected to the baby, when Kate gets home she needs to deal with a whiny, clingy baby instead of the happy, busy little one Kate was accustomed to.
➤ Because Emily is not proving to be very competent, more of the housework falls on Kate, which is very draining.

You can see that although Kate is dealing with numerous issues, the common cause is that the housekeeper is not who she needs her to be. While finding a new childcare provider may not be an easy task, at least Kate now knows the root cause of her family's imbalance and she and her spouse can take steps to rectify it by finding more suitable help. This example shows how making one change that affects a multitude of stressors can minimize, or eliminate, the majority of problems you as a working mom may face. Often when you attempt to find a common cause for a cluster of seemingly unrelated problems, you will discover that by resolving the root issue, by making a change in only one area (the housekeeper), you will eliminate or minimize many other problems.

Creative Vehicle #3

Ask the correct questions.

Nora, a songwriter for Broadway shows and mother of four, illustrates our third vehicle: the importance of asking the right questions in any given situation.

THE PROBLEM

> *I decided to take my children to an amusement park last summer. My eldest child was twelve and we had agreed that she would help me as much as possible. Since she was almost a teenager I felt she was capable of shouldering some responsibility for her three younger brothers. Relying on her to be my right hand, I also invited two nieces to come along so that my daughter would have girls to hang out with.*
>
> *The chaos began when my daughter took two of the boys to the bathroom at the other end of the park without letting me know. I spent twenty-five minutes searching for them, becoming more frantic by the*

moment, until I saw them approaching from the far end of the grounds.

After being on the brink of collapse, I vented my anger the minute my daughter got close enough to hear me scream. She was insulted that instead of thanking her for helping out, I was attacking her. The little ones sensed the tension and started acting up. After my outburst I felt angry and miserable about the many hours of driving and the amount of money spent on admission and rides. Now we were all in a bad mood during what was supposed to be a fun day.

We can certainly imagine the questions that might have run through Nora's mind:

Why can't my daughter be responsible and let me know if she's going someplace? Doesn't she care if I worry?
Why can't she understand that I had good reason to be upset with her?
Did she have to sulk the rest of the day and ruin it for all of us?

If we are anything like Nora, these are the kinds of questions we would have likely been asking as well. However, the answers to these questions would not leave us feeling good about our children *or* our parenting. In fact, these kinds of defeatist questions actually *invite* negative feelings and detrimental results. So let's try to creatively replace these unhelpful questions with more productive ones.

THE SOLUTION

A vital skill in creative problem solving is finding ways to prevent, or at least minimize, problems. One way is not to look for the appropriate *answer* to a problem, but instead to know how to ask the appropriate *question.*

Doing that would sound something like this:

> *Did my daughter know the restroom was so far away and that I'd be worried she was gone so long?*

I think we can safely agree that her daughter's answer to that would be, "No."

How about this one:

> *Did I discuss with her beforehand to let me know anytime she wanted or needed to go somewhere within the park grounds away from me?*

The answer to this might also be no, either because you never thought it would happen, or because you assumed that a twelve-year-old would understand this on her own.

Lastly, you could have honestly asked yourself:

> *Would I enjoy being screamed at (in front of all the kids) when all I was trying to do was to help?*

Of course, the answer to that would definitely be a resounding, "No!"

Through these examples you can see that when we use our creativity to be honest, objective, curious, and fair and when we ask ourselves empowering questions, we are allowing our feelings and interactions to be affected by constructive, not destructive, answers. Asking the right questions creates clarity and understanding, whereas asking the wrong ones usually leaves us focused on everything that is wrong with our child, our relationship, or us.

SEEING PROBLEMS AS PUZZLES TO SOLVE

All mothers consistently deal with difficulties and problems, both at home and at work. What if you could reframe those challenges by seeing the Park and Ride sign as your inspiration to view problems not as insurmountable or dreaded obstacles, but as puzzles to be solved or situations with clues waiting to be uncovered?

Here's a great example of how Aubrey, a financial advisor and single mom of two sons ages nine and eleven, used this sign to creatively "solve a puzzle" in her family:

> *No matter what I prepared for dinner, my sons complained, left everything on their plates and fixed themselves cereal and milk instead. I would cajole and try to convince them to eat, and then resort to threatening and forcing them. Evenings were definitely not a happy time in our house.*
>
> *After learning about this Green skill of how to try and find creative solutions to recurring problems, I decided to create a mini restaurant with a written menu. I printed out the menu so the day before they could order what they wanted for dinner the next evening.*

If they didn't see something they wanted to eat, they could suggest something else that was easy for me to prepare. They loved it! They even took turns being the waiters, which included setting and clearing the table. The challenge of thinking outside the box and figuring out a solution instead of creating escalating power struggles was liberating for me. My boys and I now see problems as puzzles to figure out and we enjoy solving them together!

The next time you find yourself stuck in a defeating pattern, with less than favorable results coming from your road-worn attempts to deal with detours or potholes, try visualizing the Park and Ride sign as a motivator to see problems as puzzles to be solved. You may be surprised by how creative you can be—and how receptive your children are to joining in the fun.

BUMPS IN THE ROAD

UNCLEAR ABOUT THE "RIGHT" QUESTIONS TO ASK

You are now clear about the importance of being aware of the questions that run thorough your mind while you are in middle of a dilemma. You are also more confident about how to search for the "right" questions instead of looking for the "right" answers. But how do you know which questions are right and which are wrong?

Maddie, a mother of three lively girls and a full-time registered nurse, shared this enlightening conversation she had with one of her patients who was recuperating from a heart attack. She was amazed at how the day after learning to ask the right questions as a way of creatively solving problems, she actually saw this skill in action. This is what the patient shared with Maddie.

> *After my first heart attack the doctor warned me to stop smoking. I was so afraid of jeopardizing my health that I didn't smoke for two months. Then I found myself thinking, "Does anyone die from smoking one cigarette?" The answer to that question was clearly a "No," so I smoked. The next day I asked myself another "wrong" question, "What is more dangerous? High blood pressure as a result of tension or to smoke a cigarette and calm down?" Within two weeks I was back to smoking two packs a day. I can't believe it!*

What happened here? The answers to this patient's questions were statistically and medically correct. No one dies from smoking one cigarette and stress is not conducive to recovery when recuperating from a heart attack. The problem was that his questions were wrong.

Had the patient asked himself, "Does my doctor want me to smoke?" The answer obviously would have been a definite, "No." Had he then asked himself, "Is smoking dangerous to my health?" The only honest reply would be, "Yes." Armed with that information it would have been easier to overcome the urge to smoke that single cigarette that led to his re-addiction.

So how do you know what are the right questions to ask yourself? The rule is: if the answers to your questions make you feel upset, angry, or cause you to behave in an unhealthy or problematic manner (as in the example above) then they aren't the right questions to ask yourself at that moment. When you use your creativity and look at the situation from a more honest and empowering perspective, you will find that your thoughts, feelings and behavior make you proud and do more to enhance your relationship with your children and co-workers.

To summarize, if you foresee that the answers to your questions and the anger or frustration you feel while asking them makes anyone feel terrible, picture the Park and Ride sign. Then use your creativity to look at the situation from a more honest and empowering perspective. When you take a moment to redirect and ask yourself the right questions, which will allow you to focus on what will keep you, and those around you, on the course, you'll find things will go smoothly. This will go a long way in enhancing your relationship with your children.

FEELING DISCOURAGED WHEN CHANGE DOESN'T HAPPEN IMMEDIATELY

Despite your best intentions and untold effort to effect positive change with your children, sometimes noticeable improvement simply doesn't happen right away. Perhaps you can relate to these comments made by mothers in the GPS group:

> I used to criticize my daughter's attempts at helping with the chores, but in trying to improve our relationship I began expressing appreciation no matter what she

did. I thought by now she would offer to help me more frequently, but so far that hasn't happened.

And

We usually, get into arguments about what he can wear to school so I decided not to sweat the small stuff and allow him to choose whatever he feels comfortable with. But things have not improved between us. He's still angry and complains whenever I offer my opinion.

I understand the frustration and disappointment of these mothers, I really do. You too may have a similar struggle with one or more of your children. Consider the fact that it may have taken months or even years to develop a less-than-favorable relationship with your child; therefore it might take more than a few days or weeks to see that relationship turn around. Don't despair or give up! In the meantime, keep the following things in mind. Are you perhaps overlooking small changes? Sometimes in our eagerness to create a pleasant atmosphere, we set our sights on the ideal. In the process we tend to overlook small, yet important changes. Think about the example of the son picking out his school outfits, does he complain a bit less often? Less intensely? Does his anger dissipate faster now that you allow him more leeway with his clothing choices? As we've already mentioned, noticing, appreciating, and encouraging small changes leads to tangible improvements that add up over time.

It's also important to remember that problems are not the cause of an unhappy family; they are a symptom of a less than ideal family situation. Your feelings of disappointment may be justified, but don't let them slow down or reverse your journey. Continue using the GPS skills you're learning and don't be afraid to try new skills. Most of all, don't hesitate to involve your children—when appropriate—to be part of the creative solution process. You might be amazed at how their involvement turns discouragement into encouragement as you forge ahead together.

SPEED TACTICS

GIVE YOUR CHILDREN THE CHANCE TO BE BRILLIANT

Many times you will face a parenting dilemma and come to the erroneous conclusion that there is no good way to solve this knotty problem. You might have given it some thought, remembered how your parents dealt with it when you were a child, or scanned the latest parenting book and after all that thrown up your hands in defeat.

A proven and fun suggestion is, at those very moments when we feel stumped, or when we want to pave the way for our children to cooperate, we can invite them to become part of the solution. We do this by describing the problem and asking for their perspective and ideas. Here's how that works.

Amara, you wanted to have a play date tomorrow but you have a dentist appointment. What do you suggest we do?

When allowing your children to become part of the solution, most often what they suggest will be acceptable to them and if you are amenable to that, it will clear the road to their immediate cooperation. Children enjoy being the navigators when there is a compromise to be reached.

Mom, I think Ava would love to come along for the long ride to the dentist. She can color in the waiting room while I am having my teeth cleaned and then we can stop for ice cream on the way home.

With a little prompting by you and the use of good parenting communication, Amara has come to a conclusion on her own that is one possible way to solve this dilemma.

ASK YOURSELF WHAT YOU WOULD SUGGEST TO A FRIEND

Many times we feel stuck in a situation which seems impossible to solve. A tried-and-true speed tactic for motivating ourselves to think outside the box is to ask ourselves what we would suggest to a friend who is struggling with a similar situation. Sometimes, because we are so involved in our parenting dilemma, we can't find a creative way of looking at the problem and finding a workable solution which isn't immediately obvious. When we use this method of imagining ourselves giving direction or guidance to our nearest and dearest, we unleash the inner mentor and wise mind we all possess and most times find, to our delight, that we are able to come up with an idea or creative solution which had evaded us until then. Try this simple, yet powerful speed tactic; you will find yourself enjoying the unexpected ideas that come to mind when you do.

I would like to share a memory of mine as a young mother which is etched on my heart. I learned so much from this incident about how children can be creative in finding solutions to conflicting needs. When my eldest daughter was three and my son was eighteen months old, I had a bedtime routine that included me reading to them from a picture book while they sat near me after being bathed, fed and in their pajamas. It made me feel proud that I had survived another day and was putting them to sleep nicely, giving them personal attention and enlarging their vocabulary and knowledge of the world. Sounds almost perfect, doesn't it?

The routine usually went okay despite the complaints whenever I closed the book to say goodnight, but on this particular evening, things weren't going smoothly at all. I usually sat between them reading from the book on my lap, but for some reason this night my son decided that he wanted to sit on my right side. And of course—Murphy's Law—my daughter did too. The problem, of course, was that I only had one right side. I took a deep breath, reminded myself who the adult was in this situation (me), and with infinite patience (which I definitely didn't have at the end of a long day) dispensed age-old wisdom. "We can take turns sitting on Mommy's right side," I suggested with a smile. "You can sit on my right side for the first five minutes and then your sister can, okay?" I felt proud that I had managed to minimize a meltdown and was impressed with my fairness. A perfect solution, wouldn't you agree?

But neither of them wanted to let the other sit on my right side first. Not only that, they both wanted to be there the entire time, not for only five-minute turns. No amount of logic or cajoling helped, so in frustration I told them I was done. I told them I was going into the kitchen to make myself a cup of coffee and when I got back to the living room, if they hadn't figured out a solution, there would be no story.

As I was preparing my coffee, I smiled to myself thinking I had done everything right and would just put them to sleep with a hug, kiss and no story. And bonus: I would have a few extra minutes to myself. Heaven! But that was not to be. Imagine my shock when I returned to the couch and found them with a magical solution of their own that hadn't occurred to me at all. My daughter was sitting in the place to my right and she was holding my son on her lap. They had found a way to both be on my right side without taking turns *and* without having to let the other go first! An absolutely brilliant solution which had totally eluded my adult brain.

I was amazed and delighted, even relieved. But most of all, I was humbled. Yes I was much older and more experienced, but that evening I learned a valuable lesson that has served me well in all my years as a parent and in my profession. I also learned to have a healthy respect for letting others find a solution that works well for them. Despite my having the best of intentions, my children had the motivation to find a way to fulfill their needs in a creative and acceptable manner.

From that day on, I thought twice before offering suggestions and found that when I first invited my children to become part of the solution, they invariably thought of something that hadn't occurred to me.

GREEN GPS SKILLS Q&A REAL QUESTIONS FROM WORKING MOMS JUST LIKE YOU

How can I be expected to compliment my child when I'm upset by how they're behaving?

It doesn't matter what preceded the incident you want to compliment your child on, or what happened afterwards. The important thing to remember is when your child does something positive, even if it's in the midst of behaviors you'd prefer not to see, both you and your child will feel wonderful when your compliment shines a light on the positive act. As you learned earlier, this applies even if the good behavior was unintentional. It is human nature to recognize and respond positively to honesty. The art and skill involved in giving an effective compliment involves choosing one aspect from all the negative issues that are irritating you and by complimenting that one positive behavior, you begin to build an atmosphere of connection and affection.

How can I encourage my child if I'm concerned what I say might put pressure on him?

When you want to encourage your child to go beyond their comfort zone, but are concerned about the resulting pressure, try assuming they will behave in the best way possible and describe that in detail. This might seem like a bit of manipulation, but it does work. By assuming they will behave the way you expect them to, you are describing without using praise, which might cause pressure. Here are a few examples of what I mean:

> *I know you just received a new game for your birthday and I'm sure that when Diego comes over you'll invite him to play with you.* [You assume he will rise above his possessiveness and share.]

> *Even though you love to ride your bike after sitting all day in class, I'm sure that when I call you to come in for supper, you'll come home quickly even though your friends are still outside.* [You assume he will leave his friends when he sees it's time to go home.]

> *I know I can count on you to understand if I need to stay late at work tonight. You know how much I love being home and I'm grateful that you try to be okay with me working late when it happens.* [You assume she'll remember this when she's missing you later.]

I'm sure your son or daughter might not automatically share, come home quickly when summoned, or accept the fact that you need to stay late at work once again. But when we *assume* positive behavior on their part, it is easier for them to imagine themselves being or becoming the way you described them. When we hear someone we trust paint a picture of us we hadn't yet imagined, it can motivate us to attempt to earn the credit already given. Try it and see how it works!

What if my children don't like the routines I have created?

If at first your children aren't thrilled with the routines you have chosen, take heart. It takes most of us time to get used to anything new or different. If this is a new routine you have instituted, you need to give it time to become an integral part of your family's daily schedule. Then, if despite the time you have allotted it still doesn't seem to be working, see if everyone has a problem with it or if the issue resonates with only one child.

Obviously, if everyone finds the new routine difficult or impossible to accept, it is an indication that it needs to be adjusted, modified, or substituted by something more fitting. If only one of your children finds it difficult to cooperate, see if there is room to accommodate that child's specific needs. If not, then you'll have to decide whether to try something else that might work for everyone involved or figure out how to help this child cope with the difficulty.

Either way, remember that parenting is an ongoing process. Each situation can be turned into a teaching moment. That means that as mothers we can learn about ourselves, and about our children, by working through any challenge that comes our way. Routines and traditions create a wealth of experience for everyone to learn from.

What can I do if despite all my efforts to be creative, I don't see change?

As Isaac Newton stated: "For every action, there is an equal and opposite reaction." In other words, everything we do has an impact on those around us. One person alone can make a major impact on any relationship. It is no different with your children. Do you think you can make them or your colleagues change? You cannot, but don't despair. Working alone to improve your parenting skills can still be effective. Your level of motivation and consistency is the key to your success. If you are determined to positively influence your interaction with your children, no matter what the problems might be and how much they might resist, you are likely to succeed.

A relationship is like a seesaw; even when only one person initiates change it affects the other. Keeping this undisputable fact in mind should encourage you to implement the many suggestions in this chapter and throughout this book. Stay firmly in the driver's seat with your hands on the wheel. You know where you want to go and now you know how best to get there.

After making positive changes, what can I do to prevent us from slipping back into old habits?

If you have succeeded in creating positive solutions to your problems, it's natural to wonder how long this honeymoon will last. How can you rely on your children (or yourself) to continue utilizing the new improved ways of interacting you've adopted?

It is natural to be concerned about the recurrence of familiar habits, so accept your doubts and take comfort in the knowledge that they might even help you. How? As long as you are concerned about slipping back into negative patterns, you will be less likely to revert to them without being aware of it. By using your fears as a hedge against indifference, you are on the road to success. Just be careful not to confuse necessary caution with expecting or inviting failure. Instead of worrying about relapsing, think about a future that is even better than your present situation. The road is clear. Press on the accelerator!

You have now completed the first part of your parenting journey. With the Green skills you've learned up to this point, you should be feeling much more confident in your ability to parent with love. By recognizing how the Green traffic signal and road signs symbolize specific parenting skills, you can now visualize and draw from them in any given circumstance. I want to take this opportunity to applaud you and encourage you to celebrate your wins thus far—however big or small—and all the wins that lie ahead for you as a parent.

IMPLEMENTING YOUR GREEN SKILLS LIKE A PRO IN THE WORKPLACE

FLYING THROUGH THE GREEN LIGHT AT WORK

Whether you run a business, are part of a large staff, manage a department, or are the CEO of a company, you likely interact with employees or coworkers on a daily basis. And whether it's by phone, video chat, or in person, how you communicate is a huge part of how effective you are in your role and how people respond to you.

As you already know from learning the Green = Love = Go parenting skills, this GPS skill set symbolizes positive communication followed by the connection and motivation it creates. When applied in the workplace it's about what those around you *hear* you say. In other words, nobody is a mind-reader, so although you might be feeling satisfied with how others contribute in your work environment, if you don't express it, they will never know.

What's more, the workplace is often filled with pressure, competition, and the need to surge ahead. While this may not be your situation, you may still fall into perfectionist mode where you hold yourself and those around you to the highest of standards. In doing so, it might be second nature for you to express frustration or disappointment instead of applauding others for their efforts. At the end of the day that ringing criticism might be what they remember from their interactions with you, which more often than not doesn't serve to motivate. Perhaps you simply expect people to do their jobs without much encouragement from you, or you don't think your opinion matters enough to express it. No matter your situation, if your communication could benefit from a boost, your Green GPS skills can be used to your advantage in the workplace.

CATCH THEM DOING SOMETHING GOOD

One of the most popular recommendations in the GPS groups is catching others doing something good. Why? Because it's fun! And even better, everybody involved gets to feel good. We seem to often be experts on noticing every oversight, while being woefully deficient in recognizing the good that is accomplished. But, when you invest the time, effort, and ingenuity to catch your coworkers doing things well, you create an atmosphere of motivation and reciprocity. Here's one example:

> *I realize that in order to be here on time, because of the snow, you must have left home earlier than usual this morning. I really appreciate the extra effort. It allowed our customers to find us here when they needed us, despite the inclement weather. This shows your dedication and responsibility.*

Keep in mind that if your coworkers aren't accustomed to hearing praise from you, they may wonder if you have a hidden agenda. In making this important shift, you want others to be able to accept your positive feedback without feeling you are manipulating them, or aren't being completely genuine. The best way to do this is to apply the skills you learned earlier in the art of complimenting others.

OFFER EFFECTIVE COMPLIMENTS

The template presented earlier in the book emphasizes what you *see*, what you *feel*, and how it *affects* you:

When I [**see**, notice realize, imagine, etc.] you doing/ being_____, I **feel** _____ [proud, happy, calm, excited, etc.] and _____[how this **affects** you].

Let's consider this example.

I realize that in order to be here on time, because of the snow, you must have left home earlier than usual this morning. I really appreciate the extra effort. It allowed our customers to find us here when they needed us, despite the inclement weather. This shows your dedication and responsibility.

By describing what you *see* (her being at work on time) and how you *feel* (appreciative), you are stating a fact which can't be argued. By expressing that your customers were able to find the office open, you are describing how this *affected* you (and your clients) directly. By adding an adjective (dedicated, responsible) or its noun form (dedication, responsibility) you are creating a professional compliment and delivering motivating feedback.

CULTIVATE AN ATMOSPHERE OF GRATITUDE

If you are asking yourself why your employees (or boss) need(s) to be appreciated for doing the tasks they are meant to do, think about how you feel when you fulfill your obligations, both at home and at work, and are taken for granted. Yes they earn a salary, and yes you take home profits (or a salary) generated by your business, but does that negate the need for recognition and appreciation?

Even if we do what we are hired to do, we and those around us often go that extra mile—whether of our own initiative or at the request of a higher-up. We may stay late, pitch in when a big project is close to a deadline, or prepare reports earlier than usual for an important client. Whatever the case, there may be an urgent need for all hands on deck. If you want the cooperation and consideration of everyone in the workplace, then begin by investing now in cultivating an atmosphere of gratitude, acknowledgement, and consideration. Do this by making it a priority to highlight your delight in their diligence, loyalty, or initiative and enjoy the results you're bound to notice sooner than you imagine.

To view this from the employee side let's take a look at Marci, a school counselor in a local high school and single mom raising three children under ten. Marci had this to share:

> *Despite the long hours and the intense issues I deal with daily, I do my best to always do more than the expected. I decorated my office on my own to make it more inviting and less institutional. I often call parents in the evenings to keep them posted and I make sure to share in detail whatever is pertinent to other staff at school. It is very disappointing to admit that the only time I am called into the principal's office is to hear a student, parent, or teacher has a complaint about me. It is very disheartening.*

I'm sure that the principal is harried, the teachers are overworked, and the parents are dealing with untold issues with their children. Yet, how long does it take to say something positive, point out the extraordinary, or simply express appreciation? A minute or less is all that's required. What is the effect of that positive reinforcement? The effects are invaluable and eternal.

If you're wondering how you can use these Green GPS skills with your coworkers or managers to further your career, keep in mind that everyone, no matter their status in the company, appreciates being recognized for what they do. Even better is surprising them by catching them doing something positive they hadn't even realized mattered to you. Add to that the effective skill of praising them for what they *didn't* do, and you are ready to fly through the green light using positive communication to create great working relationships. Here are a few examples:

> To your department head: *I heard about the difficult financial situation the company's been in the last few weeks and I really appreciate that despite the pressure you might be feeling you haven't cut the end-of-year bonuses for us.*
>
> To your coworker: *I know we have hectic shifts, but you always make sure the desk we share is neat, the notes for each client are up to date, and the coffeemaker is full. It makes it so much easier for me to start my 10:00 pm shift thanks to your thoughtfulness.*
>
> To your client: *I heard that you weren't satisfied with your recent experience with our company and I appreciate you giving us another chance. I will personally handle your account to make sure we over-deliver this time.*

Words are more powerful than you realize. When you use your words wisely to build and cement your important relationships at work, you will no doubt enjoy the benefits of motivation, collaboration, and success.

A note of caution: one bump in the road you may experience is how, when, and where to express your gratitude when you have numerous people under your supervision. If you consistently single out only certain employees to compliment publicly, it can become problematic. Sure, some might be spurred on to greater performance in the hope of catching your eye, but it can also create an environment of favorites, competition, and backstabbing that is detrimental and toxic. Because this requires a delicate balance, you will need to use your intuition, experience, and common sense when implementing the Green communication skills to enhance, not damage, your work relationships.

To illustrate this, let's take the example of Toni, head of marketing and sales in a high-end gift company and mother of three girls ages two, eight, and eleven:

> *I returned from a week at the home office where they insisted we use competition to motivate our salespeople. I devised a plan that included three tiers based on gross sales: gold, silver and bronze. This way everyone could try their best to achieve one of these levels based on their monthly sales. I found this to be a perfect solution because everyone was motivated without the jealousy and infighting personal competition usually creates.*
>
> *I credit my GPS skill set for being able to implement this at work. It is exactly what I tried with my girls at home. Since they are at very different ages, I wanted them each to earn their place according to what I could logically expect of each of them; instead of comparing them. I created a "Candyland" journey for each of my girls with gumdrops symbolizing a daily chore I expected them to carry out without being reminded. When they "collected" all the gumdrops on the path for accomplishing age-appropriate tasks, they each earned their own gingerbread house. It worked like magic! There was no sibling rivalry and I felt great!*

What's also great is that it wasn't much of a stretch to apply this same technique with my employees.

It may take a bit of ingenuity on your part, but if you make it fun and try to make everyone feel good about their jobs, you may be surprised just how good it makes you feel in the process!

APPLYING THE GREEN MILE MARKER SIGN AT WORK

By now, you are likely convinced that consistency and encouragement yield faster results and greater success than changing course too often or tossing out criticism. So why do we even need the Green Mile Marker road sign to remind us?

As we discussed in the parenting section, the obvious is often overlooked. You are aware of the importance of creating systems and maintaining consistency so that your workflow and production is uninterrupted. And yes, you realize that encouragement breeds positive results and is a proven motivator. Yet, how often do we get so busy with the daily needs of our workload that we unwittingly veer away from these practices?

CONSISTENCY AS CRUISE CONTROL

The Green Mile Marker lets us know where we are on our journey and how much longer it will take for us to reach our destination if we continue along our route. We typically encounter these signs when traveling on an open road with long stretches of scenery, so when traffic's not an issue we can set ourselves on cruise control and mostly enjoy the ride. Similarly, we can envision the mile marker sign in the workplace as a reminder that having certain actions on cruise control helps people gain more enjoyment from their jobs, as well as a sense of security. These consistency markers can be as simple as using the following suggestions:

EMPLOYEES APPRECIATE ROUTINES

To ensure a positive workplace environment, you already know that routines create a comforting level of consistency; any number of routines can have this positive effect. It might be your weekly or monthly staff meetings, your open-door policy at pre-arranged times, casual dress Fridays, holiday parties, the list goes on. No matter what you instill as a routine, it gives your employees a certain level of dependability they can look forward to. Ask yourself, "Do I need to establish some routines in the workplace? If I already have some in place, which ones are serving us well? And of those, do some need a bit of attention or tweaking?"

It's true that it's important not to let regular events such as staff meetings become mundane, but a certain level of consistency is reassuring. For example, take the celebration of each employee's birthday. When that's something everyone can count on, it fosters good feelings about the camaraderie shared in the workplace. Similar activities will affect the workplace atmosphere in a positive manner. Consider these examples from mothers in our GPS group:

> *Since the new CEO took over, I love my job more than ever before. Instead of feeling like an insignificant cog in this huge company, he actually knows my name and every employee gets a cake and a gift certificate for*

their birthday. It's only once a year, but it makes me feel special all year round.

I'm working harder than I used to, but as weird as this may sound, I'm enjoying my job much more. Social work isn't an easy profession, but since the new work rules were put into place, I know that whatever I write will be read and taken into consideration, so I don't mind putting in the extra time to finish necessary reports.

When you realize the importance of consistency in the workplace, you will value routines and traditions and encourage yourself and those around you to applaud and validate them as well. And don't forget the value of asking for input: your employees may have great ideas for routines and they will appreciate being heard—and think how gratified they'll feel if their idea is implemented.

COMMUNICATE THE WAY YOU WOULD PREFER TO BE SPOKEN TO

Many of our daily work interactions consist of instructions (*Have that report on my desk by tomorrow morning*), warnings (*If I don't have the reports, I won't be able to calculate your commission this week*), absolutes (*I **always** have to remind you about this—you **never** get them in on time on your own*), and criticism (*It doesn't seem like you're taking your responsibilities seriously since I promoted you*).

All these comments can be factually true and you might be the person who is responsible for these employees' performance. But do you believe this type of negative communication will create the positive results you are expecting? Think how you feel when you're addressed in this manner, such as when your boss, coworkers, employees, or clients emphasize only what you don't do, or what you aren't doing, when they speak to you. With this in mind, if you make it a habit to speak to others as you like to be spoken to, you will have no problem being clear and consistent in using the Green communication skill set to the benefit of everyone involved.

USE SCAFFOLDING PRAISE

Your career is a work in progress. With each passing year you have more experience, are more cognizant of your short and long-term goals, and are moving ever upward. Since there are always more heights to scale, more creative ideas to implement, and the next promotion to invest in, you might feel that it is never the right moment to compliment, encourage, or celebrate. The project is only halfway done, the client didn't sign yet, and the end-of-year profit margin isn't clear. So, what exactly do you praise?

What helps in situations like these is using scaffolding praise. Once again, this is praise that is not reserved for the final outcome, but instead encourages everyone involved as they make their way toward the desired goal. And just like with our children, we use this kind of praise at work to shine a light on what's been accomplished, motivating everybody to continue doing their best as they work toward completion. Here is an example:

I realize it takes a while to have the show windows ready for the holiday season. We still have a way to go, but so far it looks different and exciting. Keep up the great work!

I know you only started your new position two weeks ago, but I've already heard from many people in the department that they're really happy with the personal meetings you conducted with each of them. I'm impressed with your dedication and am glad you got this promotion.

When we save our praise only for when a person or team has finally reached their goal, we are leaving everyone on their own during the long, lonely road toward achievement. But, when we reach out from time to time to acknowledge and mark their progress, as the mile marker does, we are indicating—even before they reach their destination—that we are aware of their effort and appreciate them staying the course. And isn't remaining consistent, despite the amount of time and effort it takes to accomplish our goals, reason enough for positive feedback?

ASSUME THE BEST

As with everything in life, there can always be too much of a good thing. At times, too much praise, encouragement, and emphasis on what you expect and how someone is doing might create unnecessary pressure, which can be counterproductive. Instead you can try using the "assume method." It sounds like this:

I know it's not easy to take over a department with almost no notice after the previous manager worked here for over a decade, but I'm sure that with your sensitivity, tact, and patience, you'll win over our dedicated staff. [Without pressure, praise, or compliments you assumed her desired behavior and set the stage for her success.]

I realize that clients can be irritated and frustrated when we're so busy during the holiday season and I'm thanking all of you in advance for remaining calm and professional no matter what they say or do. [Here you assume they will react the way you need them to, while describing the difficulty and thanking them in advance]

You might feel this is a bit manipulative, but when you paint a picture of how you believe they can rise above, respond, and accomplish, you are actually gifting them a vision of a better version of themselves. It is up to them to decide if they want to live up to that and make both of you proud.

APPLYING THE GREEN PARK AND RIDE SIGN AT WORK

Every day at work you need to deal with decisions, problems, challenges, and difficulties. How do I know? Any growing business and career needs our constant attention in order to survive and to thrive.

You already know that the Green Park and Ride road sign symbolizes the need for finding creative solutions to common problems, so let's see how you can utilize and implement these skills to enhance your work experience.

WHOSE PROBLEM IS IT?

Many of us waste precious time trying to fix problems that aren't really ours. When we get frustrated realizing that nothing we have suggested or done is helpful, it's time to investigate if perhaps that particular problem isn't ours to solve.

Selena, a mother of two and expert copywriter at a large advertising firm, shared this with the group:

I've been working at this firm for many years and I love figuring out what and how to write so my clients can market their products successfully. I have a few assistants and we all work on one floor with glass walls separating our workspace. Lately, important clients have begun to meet with me in my office and it bothers me that they see the messy desks and the snacks my coworkers bring to work each day. I feel it detracts from the professional atmosphere I want to create.

I've tried everything, but to no avail. I've asked them to straighten their desks, to only eat in the break room, and even brought the issue to the attention of the head of our department. The only thing I achieved was creating tension and ill will. Nothing else changed. But when I learned about this Green skill in the GPS group, I realized this is my problem because it bothers me. To rectify the problem I bought beautiful blinds for my glass partitions, which I close when I have an important meeting. The problem is now solved and everyone is happy. I wish I would have known about this Green skill years ago; it would have prevented a lot of unnecessary grief.

When there's an issue in the workplace, make it a point to ask yourself who is bothered by the situation or who the problem belongs to. Then try to brainstorm creative solutions to solving that problem with minimum input, if possible, from those who don't "own" the problem. You might be surprised by how easy it is to improve the situation if you simply do things a little differently than you have before.

FIND ONE COMMON CAUSE

You might often feel like you are overwhelmed with a litany of problems; trying to solve each of them will take energy, time, and resources that you don't have—and will usually leave you still grappling with your original concern, only now you are also exhausted.

A better approach when you're inundated with numerous things that are trying your patience is to see how many of them can be traced back to one common cause.

Lisa, a mother of four girls ages two through twelve, who works long hours in her busy upscale restaurant, shared the following:

> For the past few months, I've been dealing with one thing after the other. First there were complaints about having to wait too long for a table, then about lack of privacy because the tables were too close together. This caused us to lose some long-time customers. Then I had too many broken dishes and ruined meals when the waiters were jockeying for space and dropped plates. I was going out of my mind until I realized all these issues could be solved if we rented and annexed the empty store next door. After three weeks of round-the-clock renovations, we are up and running—and busier than ever. All the problems were solved once we had more space! This GPS creative solution skill saved my business in the nick of time.

There are many ingenious ways for you to approach your work problems creatively. By using the Park and Ride Green skills, you will find that thinking creatively will create surprisingly successful results.

EASE OTHERS SMOOTHLY THROUGH CHANGE

As we discussed in the parenting section for the Green Park and Ride sign, solving problems creatively is an art based on a willingness to embrace change; thinking outside the box means seeing something from a different perspective. This may seem simple and even logical, but in reality, it is more complicated than we realize. Human beings are creatures of habit. We are used to doing things our way and give little conscious thought to our daily actions until something unusual grabs our attention. Not only is it difficult for those in charge to make a change, but take into consideration that they know their employees will ultimately be affected by this change as well. Most likely the employees will initially express strong resistance. Why? Because nobody likes being told what to do and most of us don't want to admit that the way we've been doing things up until now hasn't been very efficient. Even if the new idea is amazing, those who didn't come up with it on their own may resist, so it's smart to prepare yourself for a lack of enthusiasm or cooperation.

The most effective way to deal with this situation is to be prepared and have realistic expectations. Also, bringing up any possible resistance on your own, will go a long way in easing them through the necessary transition. You might say to your employees:

> *I know you've always worked ten-hour shifts, three days a week. But I've decided to divide the shifts so that everyone comes in for a seven-hour shift five times a week. This way, we can keep the store open*

fourteen hours a day. I realize it will take time for you to get used to this new schedule, but keep in mind that because of the new hours, you'll have more time for yourselves each day—and you'll be getting the same salary for fewer hours of actual work. So how about we try this plan for a month without making any rash decisions and just see how it goes? We'll begin a week from Monday and we'll meet a month later to assess its success.

In this example, you've done three things:

> ➤ You've raised the issue of the possibility of change being difficult to accept.
> ➤ You've pointed out the advantages, more daily free time and less work for the same pay.
> ➤ You've let them know that for the first month, you won't be making any final decisions.

By presenting these key elements of the plan, you realistically and responsibly set the stage for a difficult transition to succeed.

I want to remind you, not all change comes about because of a problem or issue. Some of our greatest inventions were created as a result of somebody realizing that although things were acceptable the way they were, there could and should be a better way. By the same token, if you have great expectations from your business or career— and things are running smoothly at this point—know that change can be positive and you can use all the Green skills at your disposal to make your dream a reality with as little fallout as possible.

A word of caution though: just because *you* are convinced of the importance of the upcoming change, don't be surprised or disappointed if your employees, clients, or coworkers don't accept and applaud the changes as quickly as you had hoped. Give them time and take into consideration that it took you years to develop the problems you're dealing with, or to come up with a new plan, therefore it might take more than a short time to see positive results. Continue with your efforts a while longer and don't give up too soon.

You may also need to ask yourself if you are perhaps overlooking the possibility that making several small changes would be more effective than making one huge change. Sometimes in our eagerness to create a pleasant atmosphere, we set our sights on reaching the ideal as quickly as possible. In the process, we tend to overlook implementing small, yet vital changes. But keep in mind that noticing, appreciating, and encouraging small changes can often lead to more tangible improvements.

If you have succeeded in creating positive solutions to your problems, you may now be wondering how long this new reality will last. Just like with your children, it is natural and necessary to be concerned about the recurrence of familiar habits, so acknowledge your concerns and take comfort in knowing they might even help you.

As long as you are aware of not slipping back into negative patterns, you will be less likely to revert to previously upsetting situations. Just don't confuse necessary caution with expecting or inviting failure. Instead of worrying about relapsing, think about a future in your business or career that is even better than your present situation. The road is clear. Step on the accelerator and enjoy the ride!

PART II

RED = AUTHORITY = NO

PARENTING WITH RED

How do you feel when someone tells you no? Even when you understand they have a good reason for refusing you, what does it feel like? If you are like me, you don't like hearing the word no. I not only feel awful when I hear a no, but I also don't like to say no.

I always wanted to be a good and loving mother—and more importantly, a mother who is loved by all her children. This might sound logical and even touching, but in reality, it becomes a problem because children don't feel particularly loving when they hear the word no. Despite wanting my children to adore me, I soon realized as a mother wanting to raise children in a well-run household while succeeding at my career, I needed to set limits and boundaries. Knowing how to do this without saying no was almost impossible.

To complicate matters, it was even more difficult for me to say no because of the many hours I spent at work. When I finally came home and had a chance to be with my children, I wanted them to be happy—and hearing no wasn't at the top of their wish list. Frankly, that was one of the main motivations behind my avoidance of saying the necessary no. In addition, I think I was too exhausted to deal with any explosive reactions I would cause by my children not getting their way. And so, I admit, for those reasons and many others, I didn't say no.

Not saying no created a reality where I would try to avoid being near my children so they couldn't ask me again for something I really wanted to refuse. That led to me walking around constantly exhausted and resentful—angry at them and at myself—for saying yes when I didn't want to. Still, I consistently consoled myself: at least I wasn't a mean mother saying no all the time.

This is how I spent my first few years as a young mother. As I was struggling to raise my growing family while finishing my studies and building my private practice, I would bend over backwards to avoid having to say no.

Needing to feel justified and competent (instead of guilty that I didn't know how to enforce boundaries), I read every parenting book, became an ardent fan of positive reinforcement, and did a wonderful job persuading myself that I was okay with allowing my kids to jump around until all hours (although I had to get that important report done). I also did a great job of convincing myself that I didn't mind feeding them every time they said they were hungry (although they had eaten a nutritious dinner and had an evening snack), and I was sure that I had no problem with them refusing to do their homework (although it was to their detriment scholastically). This seemed to be working for a while, but I became depleted and frustrated. I couldn't figure out why I was so miserable if I was doing everything "right."

If you think I was only a "no" avoider at home, I was also well aware that I didn't say no at work. I didn't want to make my colleagues think, even for a moment, that because I was a mother, I couldn't hold my own. Add to that my social and extended family obligations and I was seriously flirting with an overdose of people pleasing. Or, for our purposes, children pleasing. And that doesn't make for calm, loving mothering. The sad part was that I really didn't know how to make things better.

This is where my Working Mother's GPS system made things so much easier. The traffic light signals and road signs are very clear: the Red signal and its accompanying signs symbolize authority, or the power of saying no.

I realized that if I ever wanted to feel comfortable and capable using the necessary Red skills of restraint and setting limits for my children, I would have to invest the time and resources into understanding the importance of authority and its benefits. Despite the undisputed logic in that, it was a bit scary for me to imagine changing; I would have to become a different kind of mother.

As a parent, in every interaction you have with your child, you want to be the one who is always in the driver's seat— the competent adult who knows what to do, why you're doing it, and how best to accomplish your goal and reach your destination safely and with speed.

Yes, every mother is different and each child is unique. Your personal roadmap might change and evolve as you press the accelerator while driving on the road ahead, but the following Red = Authority = No skills will help you to embrace your role as the one in charge, while putting your critical Green = Love= Go skills to work as well.

USING THE RED LIGHT AS A PARENTAL GUIDING LIGHT

EMBRACING AUTHORITY AS COMPETENCY

As with any change we pursue in life, we need a clear and convincing mindset before starting out on our journey. In addition, we need to be aware of what our exact destination is. If we don't know where we're going, then no GPS or WAZE can help us get there. This was a very important commitment for me. I needed to re-examine my thoughts and associations pertaining to authority in order to have a clear vision of what my parenting goals were.

Part of my challenge was that what I remembered from my childhood involving figures of authority wasn't very pleasant. Being scolded by my babysitters or called to the principal's office didn't make me enthusiastic about asserting my authority as a mother.

But I realized I had to ask myself, "How are my children affected when I confidently take the parenting reigns?" The answer came through discussions in the parenting groups I supervised, as well as in the personal coaching I invested in. What I learned is that authority puts the responsibility to lead by example on the shoulders of parents, not on children. It also gives our children the security of knowing their family is being run by competent adults who know who they are, where they are going, and have confidence in the best way to get there.

This might sound simple and unnecessary to state, but in today's society where parents act as though they are their children's friends rather than admired mentors—not to mention that in the Internet age, parents are no longer looked upon as sole sources for knowledge or experience—using authority in parental interactions can become increasingly complex at times. As a result, unlike in previous generations where children were often "seen but not heard," today's mothers feel uncomfortable asserting themselves and using the authority vested in them as parents.

Asserting authority in our parenting interactions indicates the following:

➢ I am the parent, the responsible adult, and this is what I want you to do/stop doing now.
➢ I am clear about my boundaries.
➢ I have made these boundaries clear to you and expect you to adhere to them.
➢ I have taken into consideration your age/growth stage/situation and still feel it is important to say no now.
➢ I am capable of dealing with my child's displeasure and resistance.
➢ It is up to me to parent my child proactively (with my hands on the steering wheel) and not reactively.
➢ I feel comfortable asserting my authority when necessary (and if not, I am working on getting there).

Ask yourself on a scale of one to ten, how strongly do you agree with the above? Although you might feel uncomfortable (or even apologetic at first) when choosing to say no, there *are* benefits your children will reap, despite their (and your) initial resistance.

WHY RED LIGHTS AND STOP SIGNS ARE ESSENTIAL

Can you imagine a world with no red traffic lights? No brakes in cars? A world where all red stop signs were outlawed or ignored and only the color green was allowed to dictate traffic flow and contribute to roadway safety? You might be thrilled by the idea of never having to stop or delay your progress for even a moment, especially when you're behind the wheel and know exactly where you want to go, but is that realistic?

It's true that it can be annoying to have to come to a full stop when you're zooming down a street or are in a flow of creativity at work. Yet the red traffic signal is very much an integral part of universal traffic safety rules. It compels us to take a moment and notice what is happening around us; it is the way we prevent head-on collisions and pedestrian deaths. There is strength and responsibility in stopping what we are doing to check to see if it's okay to continue moving in the direction we are speeding towards. Stopping also gives us a chance to look around, catch our breath, notice the scenery, and take stock of other people's whereabouts and needs. We can all appreciate doing those things on the road, but how do we use these insights as part of our personal parenting roadmap?

WHY WE SAY NO

If we want to convey something to our children and give them the clarity that minimizes unnecessary power struggles and discipline problems, we first need to be *very clear* with ourselves, our partners, and any other caretakers, as to what constitutes a non-negotiable no. Sometimes we say no to save our child from making an unnecessary mistake, such as in the following examples:

> *No, you can't stay up all night studying because you'll have a massive headache all day tomorrow and won't be able to concentrate on the test.*

Or

> *No, you can't spend all your allowance and birthday money in the candy store and then eat everything before dinner because you'll feel sick!*

Other times, we say no to prevent a situation that is unnecessary, dangerous, or unacceptable. For instance:

> *Now is not the time to start playing a game. The bus will be here any minute and I don't need my morning more made hectic by you missing the bus.* [unnecessary]

You can't ride your bike without your helmet. I don't care how cool your friends think that is. It's just not safe. [dangerous]

You can't wear your sister's new sweater without her permission. How would you like it if she did that to you? [unacceptable]

If you analyze the situations described above, you'll notice something they have in common: We are motivated to say no to smooth the road for our children or because we have relevant life experience that we want to share for their benefit. This not only has the power to greatly minimize endless arguments, but it helps equip your child with necessary information that paves the way for them to make better decisions on their own.

FEARS AND LIMITING BELIEFS AROUND SAYING NO

Even when we embrace the above philosophy, many mothers still have a sense of fear around using the Red skill set and saying no to their children. Here are some examples mothers have given as to why they may have trouble saying no.

I'm afraid that if I say no, I'll be judged as rigid or selfish.

I'm concerned that I'll create power struggles if I say no too often and I don't have the time or the patience to deal with that.

I feel I need to justify saying no, as if I need to get my children's cooperation and permission. If I don't, I feel awful.

Do any of these statements resonate with you? Can you perhaps add your own personal misgivings to this list?

Another problem mothers encounter as a result of fear, is we say yes so often that by the time we finally say no, we do it aggressively and indiscriminately, fueling this exhausting cycle. For example:

Mom, can I go out and play now?

No! How many times do I have to remind you that we do homework before joining your friends outside!
Why do you keep asking, which makes me say no over and over?

Or

Can I go visit (friend/Grandma) on my own?

No! Why can't you realize that you're only six-years-old and it's very dangerous to cross three avenues and go out alone after dark! Wasn't the book on safety that we read together twice a week enough for you to understand that by now?

Or

Can I have a computer in my room?

No! Not without parental supervision! You know how dangerous cyberspace is today. Even if you don't understand or agree, the answer is no!

When these scenarios occur, do you find yourself thinking, "Why can't they just get it? Why do I have to spell everything out for them? And when I do, they conveniently "forget" and keep doing their thing. They think that if they catch me on the phone or otherwise distracted, I'll absentmindedly change my mind."

This may all be true. But think about this for a minute: Who is the child here and who is the parent? Can we really expect our children to self-parent themselves, internalize all our rules and regulations, and happily and consistently live by them without testing us to see if maybe we changed our minds? To internalize the healthy and wise rules of life and live by them without having to be reminded? Of course not.

Seriously, do you go to the gym, give up that extra chocolate, or pay your taxes on time without friendly (or not-so-friendly) reminders? Probably not, right?

But the good news is that you don't have to remain in a vortex of fear and limiting beliefs. Help is on the way.

IMPLEMENTING FAMILY RED RULES

The examples in the previous section likely hit home for you. They certainly remind me of being a young mother who didn't want to say no and when I did, it wasn't always pretty. This is where family Red Rules come into play.

Putting Red Rules into place keeps you from having to constantly repeat and remind your children when and why you don't allow them to do things. When creating these rules they should reflect values you hold dear as well as connecting to when and why you say no, and not merely be an instinctive response or reaction to random behavior.

Here are some family Red Rules that mothers have shared in the group:

> ➢ In our family we do not use anything belonging to someone else without being given permission.
> ➢ In this family it is "business before pleasure;" that means we do chores and homework before going out to play.
> ➢ We are very careful with our personal safety. We always cross streets in the crosswalk, we never play with matches, and my children know that if anyone touches them inappropriately, they are to come to me immediately.
> ➢ No using foul language or being disrespectful of others. If something bothers you, find an appropriate way to express your feelings and your needs.
> ➢ When you ask for something, make sure to say please and thank you.

When these types of rules are explained, discussed, and enforced in a confident, consistent manner, children are able to internalize them, as well as assess your possible response if they choose to ignore or resist them. Once you have established certain family rules, you will find that they become second nature; when your child asks or argues about an issue, you can simply remind them about the relevant family Red Rule. Usually this is enough to trigger their memory and it will greatly minimize the need for them to challenge or resist you countless times a day.

Responding to your child when you have Red Rules in place might sound like this:

> *I know you want to wear your sister's sweater. Do you remember our rule about not using things without permission?*
>
> *Which rule do we have about doing dangerous things? What do you think I'll say about you riding your bike without your helmet?*
>
> *Basketball with friends outside before doing homework? I don't think so...you know our rule is "business before pleasure" so your main job now is to be a responsible student first, correct?*
>
> *Jaden, what did you forget to say to Mrs. Smith when she gave you a new pen for your first day of school? That's right!! A nice, "thank you!"*

The beauty about establishing and enforcing these family rules is that we often won't have to say no; your children will understand on their own how you expect them to behave. Even more inspiring is to see how your children take pride in your values and choose to live their lives reflecting the important ethics you have raised them to respect and embrace. How wonderful is that?

Let's go through the steps of creating Red Rules together so that I can show you how simple and powerful the process is.

FOUR STEPS FOR CHOOSING RED RULES

Choosing which family rules you want to implement is not as scary as you might think. Remember, you are their mother. You know when you should stop them and when they are okay on their own. You have not only learned how to choose your battles wisely, but you also understand there are universal family rules that apply to everyone at all times—as well as certain rules you enforce depending on how old your child is and what the specific situation is.

As you embark on this project, I want you to trust your instincts. Connect to your internal compass which will serve you well, if you allow it to. Once you're clear about your family values and goals for each of your children, it's time for you to quell those inner voices that sabotage your conviction every time you decide to say no.

One helpful exercise is to close your eyes and imagine a morning, an evening, or a weekend that you would describe as wonderful, relaxing, and enjoyable. What are your children busy doing? What are you doing? Which rules need to be put into place so that this fantasy can become a reality for you and your family?

You will also need to consider age-appropriate rules; what you consider dangerous, non-negotiable, and an absolute no for a three-year-old will likely be very different from that of a ten-year-old. In fact, numerous things on the list for ten to twelve-year-olds won't make the list for a toddler. By dedicating time and thought to what you deem a resounding no for each of your children separately, you can be assured that you will feel more confident and comfortable following through on and enforcing what you have brainstormed. With all of this in mind, you are ready to begin the process. Fasten your seatbelt—you are on your way to parenting success!

Step One: Write a "No List" for Each Child

The first thing you need to do is to make a list for each child that includes everything they do in their daily routine that you believe merits boundaries. The reason I suggest you make a separate list for each child is precisely because saying no depends on multiple variables.

I recommend you start by buying a beautiful notebook or by creating a new folder in your digital notes. Then, write down the following:

- ➢ The name and age of each child at the top of their own page.
- ➢ At which times and in which situations you think it is important to tell them no. If you feel stuck, think about your daily schedule with each child. What do you do from the moment he opens his eyes in the morning until you tuck him in at night?
- ➢ What is a problematic situation where you think you need to enforce a necessary Red Rule?
- ➢ What is a Red Rule you want to impose that reflects your family values?

For example, sometimes you don't want them to wake up the other children too early in the morning. Or you might not want them to take money from your wallet without your permission. Whatever it might be, list the interactions or behaviors you *don't* want them to do, where they *shouldn't* go, and what they are *not allowed* to access. In short, anything you want them to refrain from doing should be on this list.

When you've covered all of that, shift to considering weekends and vacations. I recommend doing this after you go through the typical weekdays because we frequently have different expectations and schedules for those times. If you're truly motivated and want to cover all bases, you can also think beyond your normal home routine, such as trips to the supermarket, outings to the park, visiting family or friends, times you are hosting guests, being invited to other people's birthday parties, waiting in the doctor's office, carpooling, etc. The objective is to cover most of the situations where you usually find yourself having to tell your child no. Here is what two mothers discovered when they did this exercise.

Hailey, mother of two boys, ages six and ten, is a business coach. She had this to say.

> *I found this exercise very enlightening. I was convinced I was very laid back and understanding, but once I put pen to paper, I realized my "no" list was endless. I am very particular about how my house looks, even more so because I work out of the house for so many hours, and how I think children should dress, behave, and speak. I was actually shocked at how many things*

I had a problem with and realized I needed to get my priorities straight. This was very eye-opening for me. I hadn't noticed how many rules and regulations I was busy enforcing day and night.

Mandy, a single mother of two boys, ages nine and eleven, and a busy legal secretary, added.

While I was writing my list of no's, I realized most of them came from my own childhood. I hadn't even had the time or the insight to ask myself if these rules were really ones I felt were important for me to enforce. So, I eliminated all the rules I had automatically passed on from my childhood and began creating new ones that were much more relevant to our family situation at that time.

No matter what you uncover while you brainstorm your "no" lists, you will find this activity enlightening and effective. If you're wondering how long it will take you to finish this list, I suggest working on it as things come to you over the next few days. Whenever you think of something or have an upsetting interaction with your child and realize, "Oh, this is a no," take note and write it down. You might even enjoy this process. Keep in mind, this is not the time to change or implement anything; you are merely doing the preliminary work right now.

You may ask why, after so much investment of thought and time shouldn't you just implement the entire list of no's you have written? By now you'll agree that when we try to do everything at once, we get nowhere. When we are overloaded and inundated or when we come down too heavy, we might end up feeling even more overwhelmed and unwittingly fracture our relationship with our children. That's definitely not the goal of saying no and not the desired result of using the Red skill set. We want to clearly and confidently start creating an atmosphere where there is recognition and respect for the Red Rules in the child's mind, in our relationship with them, and in their daily lives. Although you may have a long list of no's, we will clarify and discuss how to implement only a few.

Step Two: Use the Process of Elimination

In this next step I want you to choose the five most important no's that appear on each child's individual list. You can do this by thinking about your personal life situation, your workload, and the support system you have or don't have. Take into consideration the babysitters, nannies, and household help you have for your children, as well as your child's personality. You will also want to note the time of day this interaction takes place and make your choice wisely. For example, knowing yourself and your schedule, consider if you will have the time or patience to enforce a Red Rule two minutes before the bus comes while you are rushing to work? Will saying no to his pacifier create a situation you can't deal with because he isn't yet used to his new nanny? In short, take everything into account when choosing your top five rules.

I want to remind you not to feel pressured. Nothing is written in stone. Your top-five rules don't have to be the most important ones on your list. They should be the most important rules for you and your child right now. Choose whatever you think will make your life easier, happier, and calmer. As you gain the skills to implement other boundaries when you feel a need to, you'll be able to create different lists and make other choices. Be calm and go easy on yourself. This is only your first try. Once you learn the key concepts of this simple universal system, you will not only feel competent to implement it easily at home, but you will also be able to make use of these skills in your profession and see amazing results there as well.

After you choose the most important five Red/No Rules, you will then narrow it down to three. Obviously, the five you chose are tremendously important to you. But of those, you want to pick the three that if not immediately implemented, would create or continue to allow tremendous upheaval in your life, or possibly prevent you from parenting and working the way you need and want to.

The remaining two rules will come in handy, so keep those as extras. As it is always wise to have a spare tire in the trunk of your car in case you get stuck; you can think of these extra two rules as your parenting spare tires. You can swap one or both of them into the mix if you find that any of the rules you chose aren't creating the results you hoped for, or once you have the first three working smoothly, you can "graduate" to five by adding these two.

Step Three: Create Clarity

Once you have chosen the top three rules you plan to introduce, the next step is to ask yourself, "How clear are these three rules to my child?" They may be obvious to you, but before presenting or implementing them, it is wise to consider what your children understand.

Take the example of Ethan, an adorable rambunctious boy who just turned five and has two younger sisters. His mother Maya, who is currently in law school, decided that in order to make life a little less hectic, these were the three rules she would choose to implement with him:

> Rule #1: *He cannot use, touch, or take without permission any knives, matches, or any kind of paraphernalia he finds in the kitchen that is dangerous to him or those around him.*
>
> Rule #2: *He cannot leave the house without permission because he has been known to disappear. He must either be accompanied by an adult or stay safely at home.*
>
> Rule #3: *No biting or kicking his siblings.*

Maya realized that if she could implement these limits clearly and consistently, she wouldn't be putting out fires— literally or figuratively—and she wouldn't always be worrying where he was. Most importantly, she wouldn't be separating siblings who had been bitten and kicked and then have to invest energy she didn't have to conjure up creative ways to punish him.

The question was, how clear were these rules to Ethan? If you asked him, would he be clear that hitting or biting his siblings was unacceptable? That he must never leave the house unaccompanied? That he was never to touch a match or a knife in the kitchen?

When we asked Maya about this in the group, she said the most effective part of this process was clarifying for herself what her expectations were of Ethan. She found that once that was clear, there was a discernible lessening of her constant tension, because instead of being worried all day, the expectations seemed realistic and doable, which gave her some hope. But, when she spoke to Ethan about the new Red/No Rules he was shocked that she wanted him to refrain from doing those particular things. In a paradoxical way, Maya found calm in his reaction because up until then, she had believed he was committing these acts just to annoy her. Realizing that Ethan had no clue how she felt allowed her to see his behavior as age-appropriate, not as a personal vendetta against her.

Once they clarified and agreed upon the new rules, Maya reported her days were much calmer than they had been in a long time. More important was that her relationship with Ethan improved tremendously and she enjoyed the time they spent together in a way she never had before.

If you have succeeded in making your new Red Rules clear to your child, ask yourself how you achieved that. Do this not only to take pride in your success, but to solidify your technique. Why? Because you're going to need to use this knowledge and experience countless times in your parenting journey. When you internalize what you did or said to make your family rules clear to both you and your children, you'll be able to use this skill time and again.

What happens if the rules are clear to you, but based on the interactions between you and your children, you realize they are not so clear to your child? This is the time to ask yourself if and how you have tried to make the rules clear. What hasn't worked? What has been well received? What is not consistent? After honest contemplation, do you find these rules and expectations are clear to you, but realize you never sat down and discussed them clearly with your children?

To emphasize the importance of rules being understood by everyone, let's look at what happened when ten-year-old Sophia and her mom, Michelle, weren't on the same page about expectations and Red Rules. Michelle had just received a promotion and moved her family closer to her new job.

Sophia had a difficult time making friends in the new neighborhood. Sophia was shy, so Michelle did everything she could to plan play dates and make Sophia's room a place that every little girl would love to play in. She bought her new toys, games, dolls, and princess clothing. She even baked chocolate chip cookies on a regular basis so the neighbor children would want to visit.

Michelle assumed Sophia knew the princess doll clothing was expensive and Sophia would take good care of it. But one morning as Michelle was straightening up her daughter's room, she noticed quite a few pieces were missing. When Sophia came home the first thing Michelle told her was how upset she was and asked where the missing items were.

Sophia innocently replied that she had given the new doll clothing away to the few friends who had come over to play. Michelle was disappointed and furious. She tore into Sophia, telling her how irresponsible she was and how she didn't have to give things away just to make friends.

She wanted Sophia to call the girls and get the expensive doll clothing back. Feeling embarrassed and ashamed, Sophia ran to her room crying and ended up going to bed without eating her dinner. Michelle couldn't sleep and she felt like a total failure; all she had wanted to do was make Sophia happy. She had actually used the money put aside to buy herself something for her own birthday to buy the doll clothes for Sophia. She couldn't understand how Sophia could have given away something so expensive or why she would think it was necessary to do so.

Do situations like this ever happen to you? Where your child does or says something, or behaves in a way that is unfathomable to you? Then when you show them how upset it made you, you are shocked to realize they have no clue why you are so upset? They truly have no idea why they shouldn't have done it, which seems unbelievable to you. But not even the most intelligent parents can predict what children make assumptions about or justify in their minds as acceptable. These situations often happen because of a lack of communication and because the expectations and rules are not clearly spelled out. Had Michelle set the following Red Rule for Sophia, the expectations would have been clear:

Sophia, listen. This is something I spent a lot of money on because I love you and because I want you to have nice doll clothing to play with when your friends come over. I want you to take good care of the clothes and I want you to make sure before everybody leaves that everything is back on the shelf or back in the box. When we have things that are important to us, we take good care of them. And remember, true friendship doesn't have to be bought by giving away things.

By taking the time to clarify and explain the rules about the expensive doll clothes, Michelle could have avoided becoming frustrated and threatening never to buy her daughter anything expensive again. She would also be imparting an important life lesson that Sophia would carry with her; influencing her as she gets older and encouraging her to value things that are worth much more emotionally, financially, spiritually, and personally.

Step Four: Repeat the Rule

After Michelle clarifies this Red Rule, she would then ask Sophia to repeat back what she heard her mom say and what she understood from the conversation. If you think this sounds unnecessary, or even condescending, let me reassure you that it's not.

As the mother you need to ensure you were clear when imparting Red Rules to your child. You may think you said one thing when your child heard you say another. When we ask them to repeat back what we said, they get to show us what we did or didn't accomplish, which they love. In other words, we give them the opportunity to either be thrilled by being 100% on target when repeating what we said or delighted to point out that we didn't get across what we intended to. When the latter is true, you catch a misunderstanding before it escalates. Either way, your child feels great about being involved in the process. It's a win-win situation.

If you're dealing with younger children, asking them to repeat a rule back to you may not be feasible. This is when I recommend that you actually draw a traffic light. You can then paste pictures next to the red light that depict your Red Rules, or if your child can read, write one-word reminders in each of the different sections, ensuring they understand which three things you've decided are a definite no. The hope is that even your toddler will internalize what not to ask mommy for, because the answer will be a consistent no.

If you find to your consternation that you only got half your message across, try to fill in the blanks, then once again ask what your child understands you expect of them. Don't worry about appearing incompetent in this situation; children enjoy seeing us as human. When they witness us trying time and again with patience, we model the life lesson that we don't have to be perfect all the time.

HOW RED RULES SAVE TIME AND STRENGTHEN BONDS

Now that you know how to make your list of Red Rules, I have a question for you: If you're not going to be fighting and upset (and then repairing the altercations and apologizing for the tears and the harsh words), how much time are you going to save?

I imagine the answer will be, "A lot!" What's really great is that you get to spend that time strengthening your bonds of love—and you get to decide how you want to spend that extra time, such as doing more things you love, having more fun with your children, or promoting yourself at work.

One of the beautiful bonuses of implementing this GPS system is being able to stop wasting time on unnecessary interactions that are negative and preventable and taking back your life. Let's take a look at an example from the group, where having a Red Rule would have prevented a whole host of upset.

Nine-year-old Noah came home from school excited. His teacher had asked for a volunteer to bring a cake decorated with leaves for the next day, because they were learning about the seasons and it was the beginning of fall. Side note: Why do teachers allow young students to "volunteer" their parents without their parents' consent? Isn't that drafting?

Noah had proudly announced that his mother baked the best cakes in the world (this is your cue to melt at his unwavering loyalty) and he assured the teacher that you would gladly bake the cake for him to bring to class the next morning.

You had a very important meeting with a major buyer the next day, as well as a long-overdue planned night out with your partner that evening. It was 4:00 pm with no dinner cooked for the children and the house in great need of a serious cleanup—not to mention homework with the other children, which had to be supervised.

What would you do in a situation like this? Well, if this were me decades ago, I would have first exploded at Noah, complaining about his volunteering me without my permission. Then I would have continued my well-deserved rant and let everyone within earshot know *exactly* what I thought of a teacher who would create a situation like this. And finally, I would have been annoyed and impatient throughout the evening, making my other children feel anxious and wasting a perfectly good evening out with my partner. While out with my partner I would have been imagining taking out the mixer at 11:00 pm and then having to wait to decorate the cake in the wee hours of the morning. Not a very intelligent decision based on the results: unhappy children, a disappointed partner, and an overly exhausted mom who doesn't know how to say no.

Or, I could have responded according to the GPS guidelines. If I didn't have a Red Rule in place at this point, I might decide that Noah was in great need of self-confidence and this would be my act of love for him, despite the hectic evening. With this in mind, I would hug him excitedly and figure it out. In that case I might (a) buy a cake and only spend time decorating it, (b) order a rush job specialty cake and believe the cost is worth his priceless smile, or (c) decide to bake it from scratch. If I chose the third option because I wanted him to feel wonderful, the inconvenience and wee hours wouldn't be a reason to lash out at anyone. In fact, I might even find myself enjoying the process because I made the decision to bake the cake.

But once this cake situation was solved, I now realized that creating a Red Rule was necessary; I didn't want this to come up again and I didn't want my son to see this as an unrealistic expectation of me—or of the world—going forward.

The Red Rule might be:

> *No projects or plans for school or friends if you don't let Mom know about it three days in advance (unless it's an emergency).*

If the same situation came up with this Red Rule in place, despite Noah's great expectations and innocent request, I would lovingly but firmly remind him of that rule and then give him a choice.

It would sound something like this:

> *Noah, I'm sure you must have forgotten that in this family we have a Red Rule that we can't say yes to any plans or projects unless Mommy knows about it three days in advance. We're keeping to the rule, but you have a choice: I can either e-mail your teacher and explain this to her so she can ask another mother to bake the cake or I have some cookies I can send with you tomorrow morning with a note to your teacher. What would you prefer?*

Can I promise you that Noah won't throw a tantrum? No. Can I assure you that he will promptly choose one of the options you gave him and thank you for reminding him of this Red Rule? Absolutely not. But I am sure that Noah will learn to trust you to be consistent and follow through on rules in every situation and that he will learn a life lesson that will help him grow into a responsible considerate young man.

The benefits for you are numerous. You get to have a less hectic evening, you get to keep your date with your partner, and even if you have to contend with your son's disappointment, you will still feel proud of your parenting skills. How empowering is that?

SAYING NO WITHOUT EXPLANATIONS OR APOLOGIES

Mother 1: *No, Charlotte, I can't take you to the mall now because I'm very tired. I didn't sleep well last night. Didn't you hear the baby crying? And also, if I drive you now, I won't be able to start dinner on time. And who will bring you home? I'm so sorry . . . I know you want to go now, and you know I love to make you happy, but I have a really big day at work tomorrow. I feel bad that I can't take you, but I just can't this time.*

Mother 2: *Right now taking you to the mall is not an option. I know how much you want to go, but it won't work out for me today. Optional: Offer a substitute activity or invite Charlotte to suggest one on her own.*

As you can see, Mother 1 rambles and gives too much information while Mother 2 empathizes, but is more succinct. It's obvious which of these mothers sounds clear and confident, but I also want you to consider which of them might have invited negotiations or arguments.

The truth is, even when you give the most clear and concise statement, children will try to get you to reconsider. When that happens, you can calmly reflect their needs and simply repeat what you've already said. This might sound repetitive or ridiculous, but it usually works. Remain confident that the reasons you're saying no are clear to you, even if they're not always clear to your child. If Charlotte still whines and nags, you can say:

> *Charlotte, I know how much you want to go to the mall now, but as I said a minute ago, it won't work for me today, so decide if you want to do something else or wait for another time when I can take you.*

REPLACING NO WITH AN ALTERNATIVE

Sometimes it won't be as simple as just saying no. Even if you are clear, convincing, and consistent you will find that life creates many unexpected and complex situations. Consider the fact that if you bend a rule or regulation you put into effect, it might undermine the consistency and authority you are investing so much time and effort into creating. When your child sees that you are not following through on your Red Rules, you will be unintentionally inviting them to negotiate or ignore the rules you put into place. During times like these, it is important to keep your convictions uppermost in your mind while at the same time feeling competent and confident to use the following techniques to deal with the situation. You will find that if you agree with only part of what your child asks or is doing, or if you want to offer an alternative, a one-word no or stop won't suffice. Here are some great options many mothers in the GPS groups have found helpful and empowering.

MAKE A ONE-TIME EXCEPTION

The rule is still in place, but for this specific situation you will allow something different.

The rule is no cake before dinner, but because Grandma came to visit from out of town and brought us cupcakes, you can have one now.

REPLACE THE PREVIOUS RULE WITH A NEW ONE

The rule was outdated and/or caused too much tension.

Your bedtime used to be 7:30 pm, but now that you're in fifth grade it will be 8:00 pm.

CREATE DIFFERENT RULES FOR DIFFERENT CATEGORIES

This helps keep confusion at a minimum and your authority intact.

> *On school days, I want you to be up and dressed by 8:00 am. On weekends I want to see you up and dressed at the latest by 10:00 am.*

By using the above GPS suggestions in situations where you aren't enforcing a Red Rule, you are still the figure of authority using your role as a responsible parent to change agreements when you feel it's necessary. If these situations don't happen too often, they might even be a positive experience, allowing your children to learn to deal with flexibility and change.

BE YOUR CHILD'S LAWYER

An effective way to remind a child of a rule or road sign while strengthening your relationship and not making them feel bad about themselves, is by doing what I call "being their lawyer." For example, instead of telling Noah:

> *How many times do I have to remind you that in this house Mommy needs to know three days before a special project or plan so I have time to say yes or no and to prepare?* [making him feel foolish and shamed]

You can "be his lawyer" and say the following:

> *Because it's been such a long time since this happened, you must have forgotten to tell the teacher that . . .* [You are assuming he didn't remember and wasn't intentionally ignoring your rule]

Or

I know you wanted to make your teacher happy and that's a wonderful thing, but since we have this Red Rule in our family, let's find a way to manage this (using the choices we mentioned earlier). [You are assuming he wanted to do something positive, which was to make his teacher happy]

The goal of being your child's lawyer is to find any kind of mitigating circumstances that can describe the truth, but make your child look good. Here is another example:

I'm sure you wanted to bring me a surprise because you thought I would love getting flowers, but picking them from the neighbor's garden without permission is not allowed, so let's go over and apologize and see how we can fix this.

By saying it this way you focus on the positive intention while not ignoring the issue at hand. This is being the kind of parent every child wants and needs. It is also setting the stage for professional success when this skill is used in the workplace (either by you or by him in the future).

Being your child's lawyer demands a certain level of creativity and good will. Sometimes despite our best intentions, our children create situations that even the most creative mother might find difficult to understand.

I will never forget the day my son trooped in with twenty of his classmates in tow, announcing they were there for his birthday party. It had been a very hectic week with heavy caseloads at work. I had procrastinated on the shopping, housework, and laundry (convincing myself I was prioritizing), I imagine you get the picture: I was in no way ready, capable, or interested in making an impromptu birthday party for anybody, let alone twenty starving seven-year-olds. But even more puzzling was *why* my son believed he could bring his class home for a party without letting me know and discussing it beforehand. Being a very detail-oriented considerate child, this just didn't make sense.

But there he was, facing me with his big tear-filled eyes and me feeling upset and guilty that I had nothing to serve them. His friends were shocked into silence as they realized there were no decorations, no cake, no music, no party favors—no party! More than my consternation at this unforeseen development, I was truly confused as to how this had happened. After rummaging through my kitchen cupboards (and thankfully finding something to give each of them), I walked them to the door and sent them home.

I then realized I had a choice. I could vent my frustration at my son for putting me on the spot and creating an unnecessarily embarrassing situation, or I could create a safe atmosphere for him to feel he could share his reasoning with me. I chose the second option and I'm eternally grateful I did.

In a curious tone, trying hard not to sound accusing and angry, here is what I said:

"Why did you bring your friends home with you for a birthday party without discussing this with me first?" He answered in all seriousness, "Because I wanted to have a surprise birthday party this year." It took me a full minute to comprehend that he had totally misunderstood the concept. He didn't realize that a surprise party was intended to surprise the birthday boy, not his mother who was supposed to arrange it for him! I couldn't believe how this common concept had become so confused. To his astonishment and relief, when the magnitude of the misunderstanding hit me, I burst out laughing.

This taught me another valuable lesson: that I needed to give my children the benefit of the doubt. Because children lack an adult's frame of reference they can say they understand, but we can't really know what they internalize and what makes sense to them with the thinking skills they possess at their age. This taught me to check in and find out what my children were thinking, instead of jumping to conclusions. It was a powerful and life-changing lesson.

BUMPS IN THE ROAD

AVOIDING NO TO AVOID A MELTDOWN

Is this a familiar scene for you?

Mom: *Mason, it's almost bedtime, so you can't start playing a game right now.*
Mason: *Awww, Mom. Just say yes to a quick one . . . you know it won't take me too long. Come on, pleassssse!*
Mom: *Mason, I said no.*
Mason: *Mom! Why can't you EVER say yes? Why are you so mean? Why can't you let me play now, just this once?*

You know I can finish it quickly! Please . . . why do you always say no? I hate this house! I wish I had another mother who really loves me!

I know, I am with you on this one. Being a kind, loving, and adored mom is a wonderful feeling; being told your child wished he had a different mother—one who wasn't so mean—feels terrible. But trying to be adored at all times can prevent us from being comfortable saying no. From experience, we know that saying no will cause at best extreme disappointment and at worst a category-five tantrum. That's a convincing reason for you to think twice before saying no.

But the next time you're tempted not to say no to simply avoid a meltdown, I want you to ask yourself my famous three-word question that I ask my clients: "And then what?"

Think about it. If you choose to avoid saying no because you don't want to deal with your child's reaction, you are well within your parental rights. But then what? Will you allow your child to dictate what you feel is right or wrong, preferable or impossible, just because you don't have the patience or stamina to cope with their predictably negative reactions?

This is when you need to consider where this decision-making tactic will leave you over time. Will you raise your children according to your values or according to their whims, wishes, and childish needs? And on a deeper level, how will they ever learn to deal with disappointment or practice self-control if you are constantly on cruise control saying yes, because that's what they obviously want to hear?

SAYING NO TOO OFTEN

A question many mothers grapple with, after seeing how effective saying no can be, is whether they are too enthusiastic in implementing the Red parenting skills. Are they saying no to more playtime because they are exhausted or because their child is tired and needs to get used to a consistent bedtime? Are they not allowing their daughter to study at a friend's house because that friend isn't a good influence on their child or because they want her at home so she can help out?

It's not easy to take an honest look at ourselves. But when we do, we might be surprised to realize that we often say no for personal reasons. We may be upset with someone or something else and taking it out on our child, or we may be reacting emotionally and impulsively instead of objectively. Once you recognize that you do this, you can stop saying no for the wrong reasons and instead focus your attention on your child's needs. Only when you are sure that you're saying no for the right reasons will you do so with confidence and love, which is a winning combination.

SPEED TACTICS

SAY NO BY GIVING INFORMATION

Have you ever realized that you could say no without actually using the word? If not, you're going to love this solution!

By merely giving information, you can make it clear—without saying no—that you can't do what your child is requesting. The magic in this is you don't have to use a word that usually invites resistance.

Here are two examples that demonstrate giving information that implies the word no:

> *Mom, can you please take me to the library?*
> *Right now, I'm waiting for the repair guy to come so I need to stay home.*

> *Mom, can you buy me new sneakers?*
> *We already bought you new sneakers this season, so you'll have to wait till the next season before buying more.*

SAY NO BY SAYING I CAN'T, BUT I CAN

Yet another clever way of saying no without saying it directly is to use the phrase, I can't _____, but I can _____.

> *Addie, I **can't** study with you for your test now, but I **can** look over your notes with you later, after you summarize this chapter.*

> *Zack, I **can't** take you to practice now, but I **can** pick you up later when you're done.*

Here you are clear about what you can't do, but are also offering something you can do instead.

RED ROAD SIGNS TO BOOST YOUR PARENTING EFFICIENCY RED ALL-WAY STOP = DEALING WITH CONFLICT

CONFLICT ON THE HIGHWAY OF LIFE

No matter how much you love your child, how devotedly you attend to his well-being, or how often you sacrifice so that he'll be happy and content, you will need to deal with conflict at every stage in your parenting journey.

There are numerous reasons for this, some examples of which follow:

- You are an adult. *He is a child.*
- You are always exhausted. *She is never tired.*
- You want nothing more than to relax on the sofa after a long day's work. *He is constantly raring to go.*
- You want her to save her birthday money. *She wants to spend it this minute.*
- You want him to have good friends. *He likes to hang out with boys you don't like or trust.*
- You are able to wait for things. *She wants everything right now.*

149

> ➤ You are unique. *So is he or she.*

The fact that you think, feel, and behave differently is what conflict is all about. And even when you work on yourself to recognize and accept the numerous differences between you and your children, it's simply not enough to create an atmosphere of love and harmony and to prevent any form of conflict between you. But because mothers constantly struggle to succeed at work and to be great moms at home, many mistakenly believe that it is in their best interest to prevent conflict at all costs. This might sound like a worthwhile goal, but have you ever realistically examined how a parent–child relationship could be completely devoid of conflict?

The following is a story one of the mothers in the GPS group shared:

> *It was 11:30 pm and the house was a wreck. There were toys strewn all over the playroom and the kitchen counters were piled high with dishes from dinner (and lunch and breakfast). The laundry basket was filled with unfolded laundry (I was still ahead as long as the basket of clean laundry had more in it than the hamper did), a spelling test that still needed my signature was plastered on the table with a ketchup stain, the baby was showing no signs of imminent slumber, and I had an important presentation to finish for the next morning's 9:00 am meeting.*

Did I feel tired? You bet. Overwhelmed? To put it mildly! I was also feeling resentful that no matter how much I did, there still was so much left to do and that I couldn't find a moment for myself. But more exhausting than all that, was being crushed by never-ending guilt because I felt like such a bad mom.

This was the internal dialogue running through my mind. Why did I yell at the kids to stop fighting while they were eating dinner? I knew they were just being typical siblings. Why was I annoyed at them for interrupting my call from the office? I know how important my undivided attention is to them, especially since I'm out of the house working so many hours.

Why, despite everything I have ever read and learned about creating daily parenting traditions, didn't I sit with them nightly and read them a bedtime story? Why did I give in and allow them to eat candy before dinner knowing it would definitely spoil their appetite? And how did I let them go to sleep (actually I herded them into bed, if I am being honest) without brushing their teeth for the second time this week?

And to top it all off, I didn't have the patience to speak to each child and give them "alone time," which is so important. In fact, when they came to tell me what had happened that day at school I told them to tell me later because I was trying to do ten things at once, but later never arrived. So here I am sitting on the couch totally depleted and feeling like the worst mother alive.

Does this sound at all familiar? Have there been times when you've felt this overwhelmed and frustrated with yourself? When you are juggling numerous responsibilities and feel pushed and pulled in many directions at once? When you are trying to be everything to everyone? Of course you have, because as working moms, we *all* have. Like most of us, you are constantly dealing with conflicting needs.

Yes, parenting can often be a bumpy road and raising children while investing in a career complicates matters even more. But when we face challenges that take us out of our comfort zone, we stretch and we grow—and believe it or not, it can actually be wonderful and life-changing to learn how to deal with conflicts.

USING THE ALL-WAY STOP SIGN AS A CONFLICT INDICATOR

Have you ever realized that we don't tend to have conflicts with those we don't know or whose lives don't affect us in any way, only with people with whom we are connected? I've chosen the red All-Way Stop sign as the sign we picture as an indication of conflict—but it's also a sign that indicates connection with someone who is important to you. You may feel the conflict is negative, but the fact that you're sharing it with a person you care about makes it inherently positive.

Though you may have never thought about it this way, conflicts clarify the different needs in your family, which helps you to know what the top priority is for each member of your family at any given moment. When you envision the

All-Way Stop as a conflict indicator, I want you to see it as a reminder sign, especially when you are pressed for time and want to invest your emotional and personal resources in what's most important. By keeping this attitude uppermost in your mind, you will enable yourself to face conflicts with curiosity and creativity instead of with avoidance or dread.

Because conflict is a consistent part of our lives, it's crucial to learn how to cope with it and to demonstrate that expertise to our children so they will be able to learn from us. Again, this is what the red All-Way Stop sign symbolizes. Knowing how to handle conflict constructively and with confidence will allow you to feel more competent in managing the differing needs of your children—calmly and harmoniously.

Have you ever noticed that most of us would prefer to prevent conflicts rather than finding ways to resolve them? In trying to do so we often decide, on our own, to forgo a need or make a sacrifice to avoid the inevitable confrontation because we are pressed for time and would rather have things flow smoothly. A word of caution: don't make a huge sacrifice when trying to compromise without letting those around you know about what you are planning to do.

Why is this not a good decision? Well, take an honest look. Is the price you pay in desperate situations often much greater than the joy you will create? Even more upsetting is that sometimes, your children would have preferred that you *didn't* sacrifice your time, money, sleep, or privacy to minimize conflict at all costs.

I know this firsthand because I lived it while raising young children and being overwhelmed with finishing my thesis and setting up my new office. Thinking back, I realize I wasted so much unnecessary energy by walking around tired and resentful as a direct result of trying to minimize conflicts at all costs.

Here are examples of that time in my life that I hope will inspire you to view conflict differently than you may be seeing it now. Take dinners for instance. I can't count how many times I woke up at the crack of dawn to cook a nourishing homemade meal, only to find that when I came home after a long day at work, most of it was left uneaten. Instead of resenting their lack of appreciation, which created conflict between us, I could have allowed my children to have Chinese food or pizza as a welcome change once in a while—and given myself a break.

Another time I told my children I would take them to the park, but I had an enormous amount of work to get done. Not wanting to disappoint them, I ran home in the afternoon to sit with them in the park, but then had to return to work in the evening. When I had to leave at 7:00 pm they all started crying. They said they would have preferred that we go to the park another day rather than have me leave again in the evening. Can you imagine how I felt when this happened? Not only was I exhausted and frustrated from running back and forth to work, but I was upset at myself for trying to be a "good mother" and just as angry at my children for not appreciating me enough! Not a very pleasant reality.

When you come to an All-Way Stop intersection where there are obviously differing needs—stop! Take inventory. Identify the need. This is a time that's conducive to clarifying life rules which should validate and reflect your personal life values. As you do this, try to find the most acceptable plan or compromise on how to move forward. And remember, your children are more creative in finding solutions than you may be giving them credit for. What's more, compromising without giving them choices usually creates unnecessary and unappreciated sacrifice on your part, so don't forget to involve age-appropriate children in the conflict-resolution process.

How do you deal with a conflict of needs at an All-Stop intersection? Sometimes, simply by saying no.

BALANCING CONTRADICTORY NEEDS

Conflicts are also created when parents and children cross each other's personal boundaries or when they try to fulfill contradictory needs. Here's what I mean.

As a mother you might yearn for a clean quiet house in the evenings, while your children have the need to let go and feel free when they get home after being cooped up in a classroom all day. Or you feel the need to know what your child is doing so that you can be calm, but she might want privacy and space, especially since she knows she isn't doing anything dangerous or unacceptable.

Differing needs cause conflict, so what can we do in situations like these? Just like when you come to an intersection with an All-Way Stop sign, parents and children both need to pause and assess the situation when it seems you're going in opposite directions. Although you as a parent have the right and responsibility to enforce a rule, by stopping and letting your child know you acknowledge him and his needs, you are creating an atmosphere of respect and calm—despite differing needs and expectations—that will enhance your relationship no matter what happens next. This is the first step toward achieving a safe, responsible compromise. To use our road analogy: Everyone needs to come to a complete stop before proceeding through the intersection; before moving forward, everyone must wait their turn. Let's look at another example.

Lara, a mother of twin boys and a daughter, who serves on the board of a high-profile nonprofit organization shared this:

> *Jon, I know you're busy building a city with Legos and cars right now, but I need the room because a therapist is coming to work with the baby.*

Here Lara showed her son that she "saw" him by describing to him what he was busy doing and she conveyed that she was aware that he was enjoying playing. When a child receives that initial acknowledgment, they are usually more willing to hear what we have to say. In this situation Lara clarified a need which would impinge on his activity. By expressing the conflicting need in a matter-of-fact manner, it resulted in Jon being cooperative. He asked if he could play for ten more minutes which Lara agreed to, as long as he kept his end of the deal; to put away his Legos when the ten minutes were up without whining or complaining. (Lara also gave him the option of moving his Legos to another room).

These instances are invaluable opportunities to clarify universal life rules for our children. In this situation Lara is conveying that business comes before pleasure; a therapist needing the room trumps the wish to play there. When these rules are explained calmly and adhered to consistently, everyday interactions become wonderful learning moments that when used correctly, impact our children's moral character for the rest of their lives.

Can I promise that this All-Way Stop technique will guarantee immediate acceptance and cooperation? Most likely no. That's because most people, when confronted with pressure to change their plans or forgo their needs, don't usually jump for joy. Children are certainly no different. But by being prepared for a negative reaction in conflicted situations, you will be able to remain calm as a mother in the face of inevitable resistance.

Keep in mind that the most important part of understanding and utilizing this GPS All-Way Stop skill is focusing on meeting the need and not on the way that need is met. It is vital to clearly understand differing perspectives and wishes, but still be flexible and creative when finding a solution to navigating those different needs. The following example expounds on this idea.

> Matt, your sister has a friend over. They're studying for a test and eating dinner together in the kitchen. To give them privacy, I'm going to serve you supper here in your room, okay?

Here Matt's mom decided that her daughter, Mia, and her friend deserved to have the kitchen to themselves since this was a study date. As such, in trying to meet the differing needs of both children, she presented a logical solution so that her son could have his dinner without waiting until after the girls were done. In this situation the mother saw a conflict and decided that giving Mia the privacy she needed was more important than serving dinner to the rest of the family in the kitchen at the same time. If she wanted to take it a step further, she could have also used this opportunity to teach a life rule by explaining to Matt the importance of studying with friends for tests.

There are often multiple ways to solve conflicting needs; the first solution that pops into our minds isn't always the only one that will work. For example, if Mia's mom wasn't pressed for time and it wouldn't make things much more difficult, she could wait until the girls were finished studying and then serve the family after the girls had left the kitchen. Either way, she is working to balance conflicting needs without becoming embroiled in a conflict.

And don't overlook your children's problem-solving abilities or an opportunity to help them grow in this arena. If they're old enough, whenever possible I recommend allowing them to figure out how they can compromise or wait their turn when faced with conflicting needs. You might be amazed by what they come up with.

BUMPS IN THE ROAD

INVOLVING OTHERS

Another sure-fire way to intensify conflicts to an almost unbearable level is if you, or your child, call in the troops. If you involve your partner, other family members, the nanny, his tutor, or a neighbor in the conflicted interaction, you will find that the altercation typically escalates to an entirely different level.

Take this scene for example:

Grandma, come see how your daughter is torturing me! Mom wants me to stop in the middle of my game even though I was studying all evening for my math test. Tell her to let me play!

In an instant not only do you have to stand your ground with your child, but you also need to deal with the possible scrutiny of your parental skills and decisions by your mother or mother-in-law. Ideally she would say something like, "Aisha, that's between you and your Mother. I'm staying out of it." But if she indeed steps in, it makes finding a solution or controlling your reaction that much harder.

Here's another example, only this time, you are the one inviting another person to help you stand your ground:

Nanny Rachel, please tell Amelia that you don't like it when she leaves her coat on the floor instead of hanging it up in her closet as I've asked her to do a thousand times. Tell her that if she doesn't start listening you won't take her to the park today.

Here you have involved another adult, so not only is the relationship between you and your daughter fraught with tension, but you have created negative feelings between her and her caretaker who is responsible for her all the hours you are at work. How exactly is this helpful in the scheme of things?

Remember, in GPS parenting, you as the mother always need to have your eyes on the road. That means you need to know what your objective is. In most conflicts, your objective is not to make your child feel uncomfortable with their caretaker, grandparent, teacher, friend, or other loved one. Your goal is for your child to realize the importance of what you expect them to do, have them accept your authority, and learn how to move on despite the disagreement. Realizing great damage can be caused by involving others in our conflicts can help us resist that momentary temptation to invite them into the altercation. Showing restraint at emotionally difficult times is a fine-tuned skill, but when you master it, you'll find it empowers you and engenders respect and appreciation.

WHEN ANNOYANCE OR DISAPPOINTMENT TAKES OVER

Another reason we find ourselves enmeshed in conflicts more than we like is by allowing our annoyance with, or disappointment in, our child to impact how we respond to every small issue.

Sheila, a mother of a ten-year-old daughter and two sons under five who travels to the orient for business every month, shared the following:

> I found myself arguing about and saying no to every little thing. I insisted on having my way no matter what it was about. I wouldn't consider a later bedtime, I refused to let my daughter go to a friend's house to study, and I wasn't at all flexible when they

complained about my dinner choices. After a few rough weeks, I realized why this was happening: it was because I was so frustrated and disappointed at how they behaved every time I was away for business that when I came back, I was on the warpath. Now that we are discussing this red All-Way Stop road sign, I realize that I'm not being fair or logical. I first need to take care of my expectations and my anger. Only then can I logically analyze when I really need to say no.

The next time you feel overwhelmed with never-ending conflicts, ask yourself if it's part of a larger picture of what you feel toward your children or in your role as a mother. Can it be that you are upset and dissatisfied about other issues and the way you assert your authority is by constantly saying no?

The All-Way Stop serves as a reminder to stop and think before moving forward—no matter how annoyed or disappointed you may be feeling—and since conflict is going to come up again and again, honing your skills around dealing with it will be productive for you in countless ways.

SPEED TACTICS

LET THEM LEARN FROM EXPERIENCE

The best way for our children to learn from their mistakes is for us *not* to create the need for them to defend their choices and instead let natural consequences and reality teach them a life lesson. See these examples below which refer to the dialogue presented above when discussing the need to be right.

> *Instead of telling your child the event took place yesterday, have her look at the date on the invitation to see for herself that she got the date wrong.*
>
> *Instead of saying that it did cost $10, not $12, wait until he notices the price tag on his own and realizes his mistake.*
>
> *Instead of saying "I told you so" when your daughter has the sniffles and is coughing after going out without a sweater, give her the chance to admit to herself that you were right.*

By allowing your children to learn from experience, you allow them to internalize the fact that what you cautioned them, requested of them, or shared with them was actually correct. Because you aren't insisting on proving yourself right, they don't have to defend themselves. This means they don't need to justify their actions or misdeeds, which gives them the golden opportunity to learn from their mistakes. This allows them to be open to learning how to do things differently because they aren't focused on proving themselves right. And for you as a mom? Letting them learn from less combative interaction relieves you of having to constantly correct them—and you will enjoy watching them use these experiences to grow and make good decisions for themselves.

LET THEM CHOOSE FROM ACCEPTABLE OPTIONS

Many times when we are faced with parenting dilemmas, conflicts, and differing needs, we tend to stick to "it's my way or the highway." This can create much unnecessary resistance, defiance, negotiation, frustration, and damage to your relationship with your child. Many times looking back, we regret that we created an issue over something which wasn't all that important. A simple, powerful, and speedy way to minimize and sometimes even prevent this from happening, is to give your child a menu of choices he can choose from, taking care to only give him options you are okay with. For example:

> *Miguel, you can't have ice cream before dinner but you can have an apricot, small bag of pretzels or a yogurt. What will it be?*

> *Scarlett, you can't go to the park on your own, but you can invite a friend to jump with you on our trampoline, you can ride your bike on our block, or you can bake chocolate chip cookies with me now. Which do you prefer?*

These examples reflect a mother who in the face of conflicting needs deftly deals with escalating conflict by offering acceptable choices. Try it, you will be amazed at the results you will enjoy by using this speed tactic as often as you can.

RED DO NOT ENTER =
SELF-CONTROL

AVOIDING POWER STRUGGLES AND
DISCIPLINE WARS

Have you ever been in the midst of an argument with your child or heard yourself threatening a punishment far worse than the "crime" committed, then realized that it all could have been prevented had you stopped in time?

Most of us have been in power struggles or discipline wars that we intensely regret. That is why one of the most effective GPS tools is the Red Do Not Enter sign. Envisioning this sign as a symbol of self-control gives us the opportunity to consider the far-reaching results of our actions.

Think about it, if a driver ignores this warning sign he will likely find himself in danger. But if he pays attention to the road sign, he saves himself and others from potential harm. How does this apply to our parenting?

We can all think of some situations where, in retrospect, we realize if we had heeded the warning signs, we could have minimized or prevented hurt and escalating power struggles. Take the example of Katy, a mother of three boys who works as a paralegal forty hours a week. As you read the following scenario, see if you can identify any warning triggers. Then consider how you would suggest handling the situation.

> *Katy was pressured to finish a report and she needed an hour to have it done in time for the meeting early the next day. She promised to give her children ice cream if they let her work, then closed the den door, hoping for quiet. Within five minutes she heard her children arguing and being wild. She tried to ignore the rising tones and worrisome banging, despite feeling more frustrated and angry by the minute. After hearing a loud crash, she ran out and saw that the toy shelf had been toppled over and all the board games were strewn on the floor. In addition, they had emptied a large bag of potato chips, which was crunching underfoot. This was too much for Katy. She lost it and started screaming.*
>
> *I don't understand what kind of children you are! I only asked for one thing: to let me finish this report for work. Why do I work if not for you? Who do you think bought you all those games? Can't you ever do anything for me? Why can't you play nicely together? And what's with the potato chips? Why can't you wait until I serve supper? Are you dying of starvation? Well, you can forget about the ice cream now. I can't trust you to do anything right. If I could go back to the office and finish this report, I would. Without me here, maybe you'd learn to appreciate me!*

Can you imagine what Katy feels after returning to the den and slamming the door? Tired? Frustrated? Overwhelmed? Probably all three. What's more, she is most likely angrier with herself than she is with her children. She probably has no motivation now to finish that report and she possibly feels like a horrible mother. Not only does she have the problem of an unfinished report to contend with, she also feels like she has ruined the evening for everyone and doesn't have the energy or patience to do anything about it.

Could things have been different? How could she have utilized the Do Not Enter sign as a reminder to think before acting so she wouldn't regret the direction she had gone in? Let's figure this out together.

First, Katy would have benefited from having a Red Rule of no snacks before dinner. With that rule clarified and implemented, Katy would have realized that in order to enforce it, she needed to feed the children dinner before she retreated to the den. This would have avoided their eating unauthorized snacks.

Second, by imagining what might happen when the children were left to their own devices, Katy would have given them choices for acceptable activities to engage in while she was busy working on her report. That would have prevented them from aimlessly taking down all the board games and creating the resulting chaos.

Third, Katy would have made ice cream a reward contingent on the above conditions being followed.

No matter what level of chaos we may find ourselves in, stopping to think before we act is a wise decision. I know that can be challenging at times: not yelling as an instant response in a situation like Katy's may require some practice. But remember that remaining calm is logical and effective and has far-reaching results. As you gain experience handling these types of situations, you will learn to minimize and prevent many of the power struggles and discipline wars that once depleted and frustrated you.

SEEING SELF-CONTROL AS PARENTAL SURVEILLANCE

Are you aware that there are thousands of hidden road cameras monitoring our driving? While this may seem a bit like being spied on, these cameras have actually been proven to be an effective safety measure. Why? Because when we know someone is watching our behavior, we are more likely to stay within the speed limit and drive more responsibly. This is how you can envision the Red Do Not Enter sign; as a hidden camera, or parental surveillance if you will, as a reminder to exercise self-control.

As parents, we need to remember that no matter how old our children are and no matter how far out of earshot or eyesight we are, they are watching us. Children have an uncanny way of observing our responses, reactions, and all too frequent meltdowns. At the same time, they also observe our moments of grace and greatness. In both circumstances, they notice, internalize, and many times (either to our consternation or to our delight) emulate what they see us doing. The fact that we are constantly under surveillance highlights the great need for restraint and integrity as we juggle our professional lives while parenting. Is this easy?

No. Is this necessary? You be the judge in the following scenarios.

Mommy, why'd you tell the plumber the sink is already fixed? It's still leaking everywhere.

Oops! You didn't want to insult the plumber by telling him you thought he was overpriced, but what lesson did your child learn when she heard you lie?

Mom, when you were screaming at us before about the mess, I heard you say #$@%! Why can you use those words, but you punish us when we say them?*

You are usually careful not to swear, but this evening you really lost it. After a hard day at work, it's difficult to watch every word that comes out of your mouth. But going forward, your children—depending on their ages—may try resorting to the same type of excuse (e.g., hard day at school, being upset about something) to justify swearing the way you did.

Practicing self-control takes a lot of effort. I certainly don't dispute that. This is why the Do Not Enter sign is a great reminder that what we say and do has an indelible impact on our children; picturing this "parental surveillance" gives us the much-needed incentive to keep our cool. This is not to say that our children should never see us upset— we are human after all, and our children need to see that. It's how we respond to them when we're tired, hungry, upset, or frustrated that can present us with challenges. The problem is that we often forget we're on "hidden camera," and simply knowing that our children learn from all of our reactions and interactions is not always enough to curb our instinctive reactions. If this is the case for you, as it's been for numerous mothers in the GPS groups, you may find the following suggestion helpful.

USING THE DO NOT ENTER SIGN TO TEACH YOUR CHILD SELF-CONTROL

The best way to teach our children important life lessons is to expose them to the desired behavior on a daily basis. When children learn through real-life situations that are meaningful and relevant to them, they identify with their role model (you) and naturally internalize and emulate your coping skills.

The beauty of this GPS system is that it not only empowers us to be better mothers, but it allows us to help our children be the best *they* can be—and the Red Do Not Enter sign is an excellent tool to help our children learn to be more in control of their behavior.

If your child is between the ages of three and six, using the road sign itself is a bit advanced (but you can still have it in mind when making them aware of what it means to have self-control). On a piece of paper draw a happy (green) face and a sad (red) face to be used as props when you verbally discuss this with your child. Together make a list of their behaviors that create happiness or sadness. Then, for each item on the list, ask your child to point to the face that describes how their behavior affects those around them.

Keep in mind that these discussions shouldn't take place while you are in the midst of an escalating situation. It is best to take the opportunity to accomplish this during a time of calm.

A possible list may look like this:

- Hitting
- Speaking disrespectfully
- Sharing
- Lying
- Playing nicely
- Helping with siblings
- Breaking things
- Throwing food
- Doing homework on your own
- Putting toys away
- Feeding the fish
- Saying please and thank you

Most children in this age range can easily match these behaviors with the resulting faces/reactions. As they do, they are taking the first step toward self-awareness. Once they see the correlation between their behavior and your reaction, you can then discuss the following depending on their verbal ability:

When Mommy asks you to share your toy with _____, what can you do to make Mommy and _____ have a happy face? What might make us have a sad face?

When you need to come in from outside to get ready for bed on a school night, what can you do or say that will make Mommy have a happy face? What about a sad face?

When I call to tell you I have to stay a bit late at work again, what do you think you could say or do that would make me have a happy face? What about a sad face?

Really listen to what they say and be aware of what skills or self-talk they use to control their emotions and behaviors. Then, point these skills out and ask if they are aware of these beautiful parts of their personalities—their inherent inner strengths.

What you are doing here is helping them see the power they have to influence their perspective, their environment, and how their behavior affects their relationships. Only when a child is connected to this personal power can they then choose to use it and create the responses and reactions you are looking for. Once you achieve this, you can then help them notice when smiles change to frowns in your everyday activity. It's a fun game where they see how what they do or say impacts others. It's also a wonderful opportunity to help them realize once they sense things starting to get worse, they can stop before it's too late.

What can they (or you) say when you want to stop the escalation of the situation? You can utilize this proven effective exercise. Children of all ages can benefit from the exercise, but particularly children past age four. This is when using the Do Not Enter sign as a teaching tool comes in handy. Simply draw the road sign, then say, "This is the sign that shows you when you cross it, you will get hurt or someone else will get hurt." Then create some scenarios and ask, "Can you think of anything to say that would make the situation better?"

Here are a few scenarios as examples:

I didn't mean that, let's continue playing.

I didn't know that you couldn't do it. I thought you didn't want to. Ok, can we keep studying now?

I am hungry and upset. I will call you back after I eat something and we can finish talking then okay?

Creating this type of role play with your child can help them learn how to stop an interaction from becoming toxic. In learning with you this way, they are using the Do Not Enter road sign to create a safe space for finding their bearings and beginning anew.

BUMPS IN THE ROAD

DO AS I SAY, NOT AS I DO

One very prevalent bump in the road is that many times, as parents, we paradoxically try to instruct and correct our children by using the very same behavior we are trying to teach them to avoid. For example:

"Stop screaming at your brother this minute!" screeched Mommy angrily.

"Now you know what it feels like to be slapped," said the mother as she slapped her son on his bottom in response to his hitting his sister.

172

"If you are going to be a sore looser I won't continue playing board games with you," said the Mom as she got up from the game in a huff.

If you are smiling to yourself as you read the examples above, it might be because they resonate with you or because you realize how often we expect our children to do as we say and (hopefully) not as we do. When we aren't cognizant of this prevalent behavior, we might actually be modeling the exact opposite behavior as opposed to what we are trying to encourage. Being aware of this bump in the road will do much to keep our behavior in check and allow us to be the positive role models we are capable of being.

THE TENDENCY TO CRITICIZE

Much like nagging, criticizing adversely impacts our relationships. Unfortunately, criticism is a prevalent form of communication between a lot of people. This is a result of unmet expectations, unresolved issues, and the naïve belief that criticism will lead to change—which it does, but not in the manner you desire.

When you criticize you destroy trust, harmony, and any possible cooperation. So why do we criticize? It's usually because we think we are right and we're impatient and frustrated with the way those around us are behaving. When we convey our opinion, we usually omit the tact and care that loving relationships require, expecting our sharply worded message to create a new reality—one that suits us. Instead, what we accomplish is creating a secondary problem: making others feel bad about themselves. This may come in the form of hurt, anger, embarrassment, or encouraging the other person to fling accusations back at us in defense. When these thoughtless words that were intended to mend an original problem cause escalation into an all-out war, it is much more difficult to get back on track or to forgive and forget. Take this scenario for example:

> Mother: *You never keep your notes in order. Why can't you be more organized? That's what good students do.*
> Child: *I like my notes like this. It works for me.*
> Mother: *Oh please. There's no way you can make sense of this mess!*
> Child: *Just because I don't do things the way you do, doesn't make my way wrong.*
> Mother: *Well, I don't see how you can call being messy "right." That's just ridiculous.*
> Child: *Then I guess I'm ridiculous. Thanks for making me feel like a dummy.*

As you can see, the pattern of criticism, defense, attack, and withdrawal is a vicious cycle that is sometimes played out time and again during the course of our parenting. As an antidote, let's take a look at the following speed tactics.

SPEED TACTICS

RESPOND WITHOUT REACTING

There will be times when you realize you are too rushed, tired, or enraged to respond responsibly to what just transpired with your children; when you know you are in no shape to make wise decisions. But you may also strongly feel in those moments that you can't remain silent because that might be construed as you accepting or agreeing to what just happened—which is far from the truth. So, what are your options? A method I've found that has worked wonders in similar situations is what I call responding without reacting. Here's an example of what you can say when you're close to losing it, yet want to say something:

> *I'm very shocked/disappointed/frustrated about what just happened. I'm too upset to decide what I want to do about it right now, but I'll think it over and tonight/ tomorrow/next week, we'll sit down and figure out what we're going to do about it.*

This statement about a future response allows you to respond to their behavior without taking a stand right then. Trust me, this will come in handy more than you imagine. Bonus: It will prevent unnecessary ruptures in your relationships with your children that you may later regret. This holds true even in situations where you need to take immediate action. For example:

> *If you catch your son playing with matches, you confiscate them. But you then tell him you'll deal with the consequences later on.*

> *If you find money your child stole, you return the money right away, but then say you'll decide later exactly what to do about it.*

By realizing you can respond partially or tell your child you'll deal with the consequences at a later time, you gift yourself the time and peace of mind to think clearly, instead of overreacting and then regretting your loss of control.

Another way to handle a tricky situation is to give yourself a breather. When your child sees you do this, they will respect your self-constraint and learn how to be more in control of their behavior, such as in the following example.

> *Aarav, I'm getting very upset because of the way you're speaking to me. If we continue to argue I might regret what I say. So I'm going into the kitchen for a cup of tea and when I come back I'm sure you will have calmed down enough to be able to talk to me with the respect you usually show me.*

When Aarav's mother felt herself getting angry, she stopped the intense interaction before it got out of hand. By modeling this behavior to her son, she's teaching him to mitigate his own reactions in heated situations.

STAY COOL IN THE CRITICISM ZONE

You are the parent and as such must always remain in the driver's seat. But what happens when the altercation with your child results in them criticizing you, such as in the following example when your child says:

> *You are so stingy. You never let me have anything I want. I don't want to give back the ten dollars I took from your wallet. It's mine now.*

First, you want to remain calm and focused. This is a complex situation because you need to deal with the disrespect—her taking money without permission—along with addressing the feeling she has that you are always telling her no. When words are flying it is sometimes difficult to remember the Do Not Enter sign and remain calm. But you can do it. This is the time to stop things before it is too late. Take a deep breath, describe the disrespect that is unacceptable to you and then redirect the attention to the matter at hand.

> *You can tell me what's bothering you, but without calling me names. I'm taking the money back right now and putting it where it belongs. If you want to discuss how we can agree on what to buy for you, we can do that once you're able to speak calmly and we can figure this out together.*

Here you didn't allow yourself to be pulled into a vicious cycle of painful communication, which would most likely end up in a disaster. By modeling adult behavior and refocusing the attention on the essential points, you set an important example. I know it's not always easy to see the Do Not Enter sign in your mind in a tense moment, but with practice, you will see amazing results.

RED GPS SKILLS Q&A REAL QUESTIONS FROM WORKING MOMS JUST LIKE YOU

I would love to begin using the Red All-Way Stop sign skills for conflict resolution. Where do I start?

While juggling work and home there are usually many areas which generate conflict. It's usually best to practice your newfound knowledge on the easier issues first. Often, in the rush to implement exciting new skills, you might be tempted to try tackling the most vexing conflicts. If due to your lack of skill or practice you don't fully succeed at first, you might erroneously decide that these methods are not effective. So choose an area that you feel isn't too heavily invested with explosive feelings and try resolving the conflict using the GPS guidelines. You will find that success breeds success. The warm feelings you will generate by being willing to solve problems and minimize conflict will enhance your relationship and make dealing with the more difficult issues that much easier.

If I see the same conflict repeats itself often, should I try to find another solution?

Many times when a problem keeps resurfacing despite all your efforts to resolve it, you may feel that you have to search for an entirely different solution. This might be because you think if the original solutions had been effective, you wouldn't be dealing with the same issue again. This is not necessarily true. What often happens is once a solution is effective, people begin to relax, and without realizing it they revert to their old habits which causes the issues to recur. At this point, instead of desperately searching for new solutions, try going back and consistently implementing your original method. Since you are now aware of where you went wrong, all you have to do to is retrace your steps and then re-incorporate the effective interactions.

How can I know if I am using Red/no too often?

Ask yourself if you instinctively say no more often than you would like to or should. You might find yourself saying, "No, you can't bake cookies now. No, you can't use your allowance to buy another key chain. No, I won't write a note to your teacher telling her you couldn't study for the test." Think for a moment. Do all those situations warrant a no? Is there room to give your child an acceptable choice or express expectations and encouragement, yet still allow them to do or try something which isn't dangerous to themselves or to those around them? Many working mothers are overwhelmed and use no to stop or prevent an action they have no time or patience for. When you say no in those situations, children feel resentful and behave defiantly while mothers end up feeling guilty and angry.

What happens if I know what I want to accomplish with my child at this point, but my partner doesn't agree and has another agenda?

Many couples have different parenting styles and sometimes even conflicting values. This is not an easy situation to be in, especially when trying to raise happy, healthy children and work outside of the home. Despite this common area of conflict, the GPS system gives each parent a clear effective method of parenting. Of course, if at all possible, all effort should be made to try and be aligned with your partner, especially on the major issues. It might surprise you when I say that children are more resilient than given credit for, and as long as you both are parenting from a place of love, respect, and commitment, your children can learn to respect the differences and even grow through them.

After discovering my meltdown triggers, what can I do?

As with any pertinent knowledge, it is up to you to decide how best to use that information. When you realize you are upset, think about whether or not there is anything you can do to make these times easier for you. If your meltdowns are connected to a certain child or certain situation, you might need to use your creativity to figure out how to minimize the difficulty and create a situation more conducive to calm loving parenting. By becoming aware of your triggers, you are shining a light on a segment of your life which is in need of improvement. Now that this is clear to you, you can move ahead with any suggestion you feel would make things better. Don't be afraid to try different options. And remember, don't overlook your children's creative problem-solving skills. Once you have identified your trigger, try inviting them to be part of the solution. Working together to improve your relationship is always beneficial. Try it and see what you come up with.

Are there any pitfalls to responding without reacting?

This is one of the speed tactics that mothers love best. Buying time until you decide what you want to do makes it much more likely you will come up with an appropriate response which will teach your child a necessary life rule, without hurting your relationship. But keep in mind, if you don't follow through on your delayed reaction (bought time), you will be teaching your children that you cannot be taken seriously and your original response was an empty threat. So, make sure to follow up and implement any subsequent consequences as quickly as possible.

Leaving too much time between the incident and your reaction will minimize the effect it has on your child. Instead of creating an opportunity to respond appropriately, you will diminish your eventual response and their possibility of growing from the interaction. By remembering this important step, you will be able to utilize this Red skill and enjoy parenting your children with confidence and clarity.

You have now completed the second part of your parenting journey. You have clarified and internalized what the concept of parenting with authority is and can now recognize how the universal red traffic signal and road signs symbolize certain important parenting skills which will add much to your competence, both with your children and in the workplace.

IMPLEMENTING YOUR RED SKILLS LIKE A PRO IN THE WORKPLACE

DEALING WITH RED LIGHT BUMPS IN THE ROAD AT WORK

How can you use the Red skills described above with your boss, co-workers, or clients? How can you utilize the Red = Authority = No skills you've mastered to enhance your workplace environment?

As in parenting, many of us aren't comfortable setting boundaries or saying no at work. If we are the boss, supervisor, CEO, or business owner, we don't want to seem rigid, controlling or uncaring. If we are dealing with others we may fear being labeled as selfish, uncooperative, or incompetent.

So before implementing any or all of the above-mentioned Red skills at work, spend some time first changing your mindset and becoming more comfortable being assertive. Practice with your friends or family and even write a script if that will give you the clarity and confidence you need before embarking on this exciting change.

Keep in mind that when you communicate your needs, expectations, or boundaries it needs to be done with clarity and conviction. This will ensure you will be much more successful being assertive instead of sounding hesitant or offering explanations and apologies.

BUFFERING CHANGE AND INITIAL RESISTANCE

When you say no to your colleagues, clients or department head, make sure that you feel comfortable and confident with what you have decided. Don't be intimidated by their initial resistance. Nobody likes to hear the word no. Most of us don't find it easy to deal with change. When you say no or enforce a boundary that is new, it will affect the workflow of those around you. Be compassionate and realistic. Expect and accept their reaction, but don't allow it to weaken your resolve to make necessary changes.

> Co-worker: *I am really upset that you won't be coming in on weekends starting in September. You always agreed to take those shifts up until now!*
> You: *I know that up until now I have always come in on weekends. That's why I am letting you know far enough ahead that starting in September I won't be coming in on weekends. I already discussed it with our manager and she promised to help figure out the new schedule going forward. I hope everything will work out fine.*

No need to argue. No reason to explain. Just calmly and clearly repeat what you won't do any more. You can mention other people who are involved in the solution (the manager) if there are any. If not, then practice feeling comfortable in the face of inevitable resistance.

Darcy, a buyer for a large clothing chain and a single mom raising three children on her own, felt proud that she was able to be assertive with her manger.

> *Beginning next month, I will only be traveling for two days every other week. Let's sit down to decide what our most urgent objectives are so that we can plan my buying trips accordingly.*

She came across as assertive about what she will and won't do. She is clear about when she will begin this new schedule and offers to figure out a solution beneficial to the company. Clear, assertive and concise.

Compare that to:

> *Ummm, I think I won't be able to take so many trips in the future. I really am....well.... overwhelmed and hardly see my children and besides, that wasn't what we discussed when I joined the company. I am so very sorry to make this mess, but am not sure how I can continue like this much longer.*

Here she sounds hesitant, apologetic, and unclear as to what she means and when the change will occur. A boss might find this confusing and be annoyed and concerned hearing that she is overwhelmed and can't manage her work/life balance. Definitely not helpful when considering her for a promotion or giving her a letter of reference if they decide the company can't abide by this new schedule.

APPLYING RED LIGHT SPEED TACTICS AT WORK

USING MULTIPLE STRATEGIES FOR A SUCCESSFUL EXCHANGE

When dealing with uncomfortable situations at work which necessitate setting new boundaries, remember to implement the helpful Red skill of being their lawyer.

Noa, a mother of two and proud owner of a bustling café, needed her dedicated employees to work overtime during the holiday season. Though her servers consistently gave special attention to their regulars and were usually punctual and reliable, during the holiday weeks they would create stress for Noa with their constant complaints and disruptive absences. This year to avoid the extra stress, she used the Red GPS skills at work.

> *Once again, we will need to make a work schedule which will include many hours of overtime. I know that you have busy lives and have even more personal obligations at this time of year, but I know you will do your best, despite the holidays, to make sure the café succeeds.* (She was their lawyer).
>
> *All of you are important to me and to our loyal customers. I know working overtime these six weeks is asking a lot of you. I can't exempt anyone from the new schedule because that would create an uncomfortable working environment* (giving information instead of saying no). *I **can** assist with trying to work out which days are best for you to stay later.* (She said what she could do).

We discussed this issue during your first work interview and you assured me you could work extra hours during these weeks, so I will take any unexpected absences to mean that you have decided to no longer work at the cafe. (Clear about the outcome).

By using these skills to help her be clear, assertive, and fair, Noa was able to create an atmosphere of understanding, respect, and appreciation. What's more, she had the most fun and profitable season since she opened the shop five years earlier.

IMAGINE YOURSELF ON HIDDEN CAMERA

As suggested, imagine you are being recorded on hidden camera. Then ask yourself what you wish your boss would tell you in a similar situation. The next time you are disrespected or disappointed at work, imagine you are being broadcast live.... and allow those visions to inspire your most mature response. This will enable you to have more control over your emotions and your reactions.

RESPOND WITHOUT REACTING

Another effective and helpful tactic that can prevent much unnecessary heartache is by learning how to respond without reacting. Say something that lets others know how upset you are while postponing a decision or a consequence. By now you are using this strategy in your parenting with great success, so feel free to apply it as often as necessary in your workplace.

Vicky, mother of a daughter and a corporate event planner, shared the following:

My staff are trusted and experienced. We have worked together for the past few years. Together we have organized very successful events and retreats for my high-end corporate clients. Recently two of my assistants were slacking off and the business was suffering as a result. I was extremely upset. After getting off the phone with a valued client who complained about our last conference, I stormed into their office and was ready to explode. I am grateful that at the last moment I remembered the Red GPS skill of responding without reacting. Instead of shaming them or firing them both, I let them know that I was too upset to deal with it then and that I would decide how to handle their unacceptable behavior when I calmed down. The next day both employees initiated a meeting where they took full responsibility for their negligence and offered not only to call the client and find a way to make it up to them, but to work overtime at no extra cost for the next few weeks.

I can't imagine what would have happened had I laid into them instead of using this valuable skill which prevents escalating an already tense situation to the point of no return. I might have felt vindicated, but likely would have ended up with two valuable assistants quitting, leaving me scrambling for new manpower. This would have set me back months. I highly recommend practicing this skill so that it can save you costly mistakes both at home and in your business.

Succeeding in your business or profession is the reason you leave your children each morning and go to work. It isn't easy closing the door behind you and commuting to a place that demands the best of your talents, ingenuity, and competence knowing your children are waiting for you at home. In your quest to succeed you want things to be perfect, to be done the way you think is best. When you are responsible for the results and feel those around you are under-performing, you might resort to nagging or criticizing. Most times when you nag, criticize or reprimand, people will take offense, learn to ignore your constant criticism, or resist and respond negatively. None of these reactions are beneficial for you or your work. Let's see how you can apply Red skills when you want to succeed, despite being dissatisfied at work.

CREATE RED RULES IN THE WORKPLACE

As suggested, when we described creating family Red Rules, once you are clear about what you can and will tolerate at work, it is very helpful to create Red Rules there too. That way everyone is clear about the expectations and you don't have to re-invent the wheel time and again. If you are in a position of authority you can create the important rules and then, either open them for discussion or present them to your employees as the new workplace mission statement.

Manager: *Beginning next month all weekly reports must be on my desk no later than Thursday at noon and any planned vacations will have to go through me, not the HR department.*

If you are currently in a workplace where you have little or no say in deciding such matters, create a list of Red Rules for yourself so you can be clear which "red lines" you don't want to cross.

You: *Beginning next week, I need to know about any scheduling changes 48 hours in advance so that I can set up childcare. I also need to be home during my son's winter vacation and am willing to cover for anyone the week before and after.*

APPLYING THE ALL-WAY STOP SIGN AT WORK

As a working mother, you are no stranger to conflict. Not only do you feel torn and conflicted juggling work and home, but in your workplace there are many conflicting needs and expectations to deal with. Using the many insights and skills symbolized by the Red All-Way Stop Sign will go a long way in improving your work environment even when there are many differing needs.

Many conflicts can be minimized, and sometimes prevented, if there are clear rules and expectations covering as many work issues as possible. When your workmates know what is expected of them and what you can deliver, there is much less room for misunderstanding and conflict.

Sidney, recently remarried and new at the job in the city she just relocated to, shared this:

> *I was thrown into my position as department manager because of my extensive experience in my previous job. After seeing how the GPS skills gave me the much-needed confidence to parent my husband's children, I decided to use the same skills at work.*
>
> *On my first day I invited everyone to a meet and greet with coffee and pastries. There I outlined my vision for our department and handed out a printed list of eight cardinal rules I felt were vital for our*

success. I asked everyone to take time to read it at home before commenting, in hopes of preventing a mass uprising.

To my surprise, over the next few days, not only were there hardly any complaints, but many of the fifty people in the department expressed appreciation for the clarity and even suggested additional rules to add. Now they knew what was expected of them and what they could expect from me. It minimized unnecessary conflicts and created an atmosphere of cooperation. By using many of the Red skills, I got off to a very good start at work and was able to devote more of my energies to my new family.

Had any of the staff responded negatively, I was well equipped. I had done everything I could to minimize discontent and I was a pro at delaying my response when faced with extreme resistance.

When you are comfortable letting people learn from their experiences and are cognizant of the fact that their initial reactions might be exaggerated and don't warrant an immediate response, you will be better equipped to deal with conflict, no matter what the cause.

AVOID INVOLVING OTHERS IN THE CONFLICT

Especially important in the work place is being very cautious about involving others in the conflict unless absolutely necessary. The work environment is stressful as is and creating unwarranted escalation can do more harm than good.

Kelly, a mother of four and a hedge-fund manager, had this to say:

> *I work in a large firm and there are constantly issues that need to be dealt with. When we are busy with a big client, it's all hands-on-deck. When some people shirk responsibility or put the blame on others, it causes tremendous ill will.*
>
> *Not long ago a new co-worker decided to share her complaints with one of the senior partners instead of speaking it over with her co-worker first. That caused immediate repercussions, which as a result HR began an investigation. After months of unnecessary in-house bickering, some of us were fired and others demoted, most of it totally unnecessary.*
>
> *Everyone lost out including the hapless clients. All this could have been resolved had she spoken over her grievances with the girl she was working with instead of immediately taking the conflict to the senior partners. Had this new recruit been familiar with the GPS skills, she would have had many more constructive options to choose from. What a waste of time and resources for nothing.*

Not only is it prudent to be aware of the negative results of involving those that don't need to be part of the conflict in the workplace, but equally as important is how you apply your GPS skills pertaining to compromise that you practiced with your children.

CHOOSE SACRIFICE AND COMPROMISE WISELY

You surely remember the examples I gave when discussing what happens if you say yes instead of no, when you make a big sacrifice without checking to see if it is necessary or would even be appreciated. In the workplace this is even more crucial, because when you invest more time or energy in your career it takes away that precious commodity of time with your family. So the sacrifice is twofold.

See what Lisa, a mother of twin toddlers and a senior partner in an insurance firm, had to say:

> I will never forget last year at work when I thought I was collapsing. I hadn't slept through the night since the twins were born and I was coping with changes at work due to downsizing. In my misguided attempt to impress my partners (in hindsight, I now realize that I was trying to prove my being a new mother didn't detract from my loyalty to the firm) I suggested I forgo the yearly bonus because of the new financial reality. That meant that I had to cut down drastically on my household help, which caused serious stress and pressure in my life. I was constantly exhausted and forced myself to function despite walking around in a fog. Imagine my shock and consternation a year later when my partners shared that they hadn't thought that my sacrifice was at all necessary. They had factored in

the bonuses before the downsizing and were surprised I had even suggested giving it up that year.

So all those months of difficulty which almost caused me a breakdown, could have been prevented had I simply discussed with them if it would be necessary, or even appreciated, before deciding to make this sacrifice on my own. I feel like kicking myself every time I think about it. What a life lesson learned the hard way.

In light of the above, remember the price you pay when you say yes instead of saying no. Even if it isn't you who has unilaterally decided to make an unnecessary sacrifice, but you are being asked to agree or compromise despite the inconvenience, remember how to be clear and stay strong. Keep in mind that most times saying yes when you want or need to say no, will usually not end well.

In our enthusiasm and haste to prevent or minimize conflicts at work, we often find ourselves agreeing and compromising too often. Not always is that beneficial for us or for those around us. So, the next time you are faced with a conflict of needs, take the time to thoroughly analyze the various aspects of the issue before saying yes.

If you discover that saying yes won't work for you or your family, you can always invite your colleagues, employees or managers to become part of the solution. That gives them the opportunity to express themselves, realize the problem (instead of proving to you there isn't one) and be committed to the solution they suggested. For example, you may have an issue with employees using computers for inappropriate activity. You might say:

We have an issue with employees shopping and using social media during work hours. Management wants to monitor all computer activity, what do you think?

Your employees may feel threatened and angry by this new rule and respond with:

Monitoring all computer activity will create an atmosphere of a police state. Maybe we can have periodic inspections like in professional sports. Anyone who is caught using the computers on work time for personal enjoyment can be docked that day's wages.

Likely they do not realize it, but your employees just used one of the GPS skills. It may not be a solution you approve of, but they voiced their resistance and offered a possible solution. They have seen you model this skill and unknowingly have integrated it into their communication patterns. See, it really does work!

One of my personal coaching clients, a department head, shared the above example with me during one of our weekly coaching phone calls. She was astonished they had come up with a suggestion that she never would have thought of proposing, but even more so, that management had loved the idea as well. The result was a noticeable improvement in production and the realization that all of the employees were on board with the solution. This is what using the GPS skills at work is all about.

Obviously, if your workplace is rife with conflict or your profession causes you to constantly choose between important needs, you would benefit by getting professional advice. Sometimes it isn't an issue of conflict resolution; it might be more of a recurring problem which needs to be addressed. Vetting different mechanics to find the right one to repair your car can be endless and unproductive. Settling on the right one, or otherwise identifying the source of the problem is the first step towards the results you want and need.

APPLYING THE DO NOT ENTER SIGN AT WORK

Your co-workers might be driving you up a wall. Your employees sometimes exasperate you. Your boss might be in the habit of pushing your buttons on a daily basis. This has been the reality in many workplaces since the beginning of time. How can you use the Red Do Not Enter skills to make it easier for you to succeed in your career?

The first step is to be self-aware. What are the issues, the people, or the situations that contribute to your feeling stressed out, upset, impatient and irritable? It goes without saying, that when you are out of control, it is very unlikely that you will be able to be effective or demonstrate leadership qualities in a manner that befits your position.

STAY FOCUSED WHILE BEING CRITICIZED

Just as our children sometimes say hurtful things in the throes of an argument, this can occur in the workplace as well. Have you ever had someone blow up at you at work? Consider if a co-worker said this to you:

> *You never care about any of your co-workers! You agree to everything management asks of you, which makes it much harder for any of us to get concessions from them. You are selfish and don't know how to be a team player.*

197

Whether what they accused you of is true or not, it hurts that they think this way about you. It is very easy to defend (you do care about your coworkers and you don't think you are selfish) or to attack (they annoy management which impacts you negatively). Instead, remind yourself of the GPS Red skill set you have internalized by now and respond to the issue at hand. You could respond with:

> *I hear that you aren't happy with me agreeing to what management asks of us. I love my work here and enjoy every minute I spend on these projects. I never meant to hurt you in any way.*

Here you didn't argue, defend, or counter attack. You didn't allow this hurtful exchange to impact your relationship with your co-workers, which would cause difficulty or perhaps, be impossible to rectify. What you did was to remain focused on what their issue was, agreeing to management's requests. By responding in a calm restrained manner and addressing their concerns, you are modeling leadership qualities, of which you can be proud.

Does this mean that by doing so you will make those around you happy? Not necessarily...but that isn't your job. By using the Red GPS skills at work, you are able to stay in control of your behavior and remain in the driver's seat at all times. This by itself is a tremendous advantage, because when doing so you will only have to deal with the many complex issues at work and not have to spend valuable time and effort attempting to patch up damaged workplace relationships.

ASK TWO IMPORTANT QUESTIONS

Whenever you feel about to explode, ask yourself these two questions first. What is the main message I want to impart? What is the most positive way I can communicate this so it will be heard and accepted? The answers to these questions will assist you in your journey towards professional success. Read the examples below to see what others have shared and consider how you can apply these at work. Keep in mind the dangers of nagging and criticizing.

> Nagging: *Why are you never on time? How many times have I stressed the importance of getting to work by 9:00 am and responding to all emails from clients that have accumulated since you left work yesterday? No matter what I tell you nothing helps!*

> Criticism: *Your report is a disappointment and below par. After waiting so long, I was counting on it being worth the wait. It doesn't seem like you understand the responsibility of your position in this firm.*

If you realize that your children don't improve when you nag or criticize, then surely it won't be more effective in the workplace.

If you find that nothing improves, despite your efforts using these Red GPS skills, then it might be time for you to consider other options.

What happens when it is *you* who is being criticized? Whether it is a colleague or a boss expressing their displeasure, it is never pleasant. When trying not to lose control and stop yourself from veering into the Do Not Enter zone, you will find it helpful to remain focused on the issue at hand instead of responding to the painful emotions triggered by criticism.

By using the various Red GPS skills you have internalized and implemented with your children, you can enhance and improve your work environment more than you ever imagined. Practice these tried-and-true strategies and skills to negotiate the often-treacherous highways of your personal and professional life.

PART III

YELLOW = TRUST = SLOW

PARENTING WITH YELLOW

Who do your children trust the most in the world? Who do they turn to when something is weighing on their hearts? Hopefully that person is you. And what about you? Do you trust your children? When you expect them to do something, can you rely on them to follow through?

When I say the word trust, what comes to your mind? If you close your eyes and think of the one person you trust implicitly, what does this person have or do that other people who didn't make your trust list don't?

I'd venture to say that in most cases, people who earn our trust are consistently competent and honest, mean what they say, are emotionally stable, and give us the feeling they have our best interests in mind. Would you agree?

If so, then you probably think that devoted, responsible mothers would do these things automatically; we all want what's best for our children and we try to be honest, emotionally stable, and there for them always. But the truth is we're human and sometimes we have shortcomings in these areas. When this is true, children can find it difficult to trust their parents. But the Yellow light segment of this book is all about helping you gain that much-needed trust—even when you might need to put forth some extra effort to make that a reality. If you already have a solid amount of trust with your children, the following will help you maintain and strengthen it.

USING THE YELLOW LIGHT AS A PARENTAL GUIDING LIGHT

The final element of the Working Mother's GPS system is the Yellow traffic signal. This symbolizes caution and trust. The yellow light indicates that the green signal is changing to red and is leaving it up to you, the driver or pedestrian, to assess the situation and decide to either slow down and stop or speed up and "make the light."

Allowing us to be the arbiters of this decision when we encounter an intersection on the road is actually a gift of trust. It sends us the encouraging message that we are capable of making this split-second decision while in a fast-moving vehicle and deciding on a behavior we know will ensure the safety of those around us. When we are given this gift of trust we usually do all in our power to be worthy of it. When our children are given the gift of trust, they too usually behave in a manner that allows them to continue being trusted.

As a parent it's important to view the Yellow = Trust = Slow as a two-way street. We, as parents, must demonstrate the capabilities of acting in ways that earn our children's trust. Then, it is our job to utilize daily interactions to model this skill so that our children can earn our trust while becoming confident enough to trust themselves.

What does it mean to behave in a manner that creates trust? As parents we are constantly making decisions; many of them instantaneously, which impact our relationships with our children and also the way they view themselves. This is something important to consider every time we encounter a yellow traffic signal.

On the road as we approach a yellow light—where we have mere seconds to check our mirrors and assess other cars and pedestrians—we often have only a few seconds to make important decisions concerning our children. While you now have various Green and Red skills to help you do this effectively, you nonetheless are constantly faced with decisions that affect your children's trust in you, which is why we devote an entire section of this book to this skill.

MASTERING THE ART OF ASSESSING AND DECIDING

Using your invaluable driving experience, which by now is second nature to you, let's apply it to enhancing how you use the component of trust in your parenting. Assessing and deciding what to do as a parent isn't always easy, so in those times when an answer isn't immediately apparent, I recommend asking yourself the following "wh" questions as you assess the situation:

Who is involved and **whom** will this effect?

What are my immediate options?

Which option is the safest (personally, emotionally, financially, etc.) for all those concerned in this specific situation?

While this may seem like a lot to consider in a short period of time, think about the fact that this who/what/

which checklist is exactly what any responsible driver instinctively reviews when hurtling toward a yellow light at an intersection. In mere seconds, we assess the caution that the yellow signal indicates. The same holds true in situations with our children.

Allison, a Wall Street trader and mother of a twelve-year-old daughter and two-year-old son, shared the following:

> At first I was puzzled when we spoke about the Yellow signal and how it pertains to our parenting skills. I felt that the Red skills and a healthy dose of love were all I really needed to be the mother I had always wanted to be. But then I realized that the Yellow skills were even more important because they are so easy to overlook. Just that week my daughter, Layla, had taken on a class project which was way beyond her capabilities. She asked me what I thought about the project and as we were talking it dawned on me that this was a perfect opportunity to apply my newly learned Yellow skills.
>
> We assessed the situation together and made a list of advantages and disadvantages. Once things were clarified, I encouraged her to make the decision that would work best for her. I was surprised and proud that she contacted the teacher and arranged for a role with less responsibility that would be more enjoyable and not so overwhelming. This was an amazing opportunity for her to trust me not to make the decision for her and a wonderful chance for her to cope on her own, thereby enhancing her self-confidence. I now

love the Yellow GPS skills and look forward to future opportunities to apply them.

Though Allison didn't need to make a split second decision here, she used the components of the Yellow light skills to help her daughter make a thoughtful decision. Allison asked herself *who* was involved and who would be affected. She realized it was Layla, as well as her teacher and classmates, who would be affected by the commitment Layla had impulsively signed up for, so she helped Layla clarify *what* her options were and encouraged her to decide on her own what she preferred doing. This created a loving safe atmosphere for her daughter and gave her the needed encouragement to take a necessary step, which did wonders for her self-esteem.

Now let's listen to how Olivia, the founder of a chain of exclusive hair salons and a mother of three boys under the age of seven, chimed in:

I actually was THRILLED to learn about the yellow option. All I have been doing since my oldest started climbing on counters and running around is saying no in a thousand different variations. By using the Yellow GPS skills of assessment, the who/what/which questions, I learned to decide which behaviors should even rate a response from me and why. I was also able to point out to my children what the problem was and allowed them to decide certain things on their own. For example, when my five-year-old grabbed a bag of cookies without permission and polished it off with his brothers, I explained to them how now they had no appetite for dinner (which I didn't serve them that evening) and why they would be missing a snack the next day in school. They have never done this again. They have conjured up many other exciting situations, but each time I clarify and give choices and surprisingly they usually choose acceptable behavior.

What I like about this is that I have a clear set of skills on how to respond to many behaviors that don't qualify as dangerous or rate an immediate no. The Yellow skills help cover all bases so as a parent of three active boys, I always know what to do, when to do it, and how to do it.

Both Allison and Olivia used the Yellow assessment skills before responding to their children. After experiencing constant conflicts with her three lively sons, Olivia wasn't happy being the police and shouting "stop" all the time. By utilizing the Yellow skills, she found she could easily point out *who* was affected by what they were doing and then either decide *what* the consequences would be, or allow them to decide for themselves what their options were.

THREE SUPERB WAYS TO SUPPORT YOUR CHILD'S DECISION-MAKING PROCESS

What happens if despite these assessment skills your child still doesn't make the choice you hoped they would? If Layla had chosen to remain with her overwhelming project, her mother might have suggested she think it over once again. Then, if Layla was still adamant, she would accept her decision and realize that the resulting pressure and difficulty would teach her a life lesson.

If Olivia's sons had chosen to repeat their behavior, she would have realized they weren't yet capable of choosing the healthy option. As a solution she could stop buying big bags of cookies or put them somewhere out of reach until the boys were old enough to make the right decision.

As working mothers we have much less time in which to parent our children. The hours we do have with them are precious and priceless. So when we can utilize skills which put many Red/no situations into the Yellow/slow category instead, it relieves us from having to be constant naysayers and creates opportunities for our children to learn how to choose, decide, and deal with the natural consequences of their decisions. How wonderful is that? These Yellow (not Red/not Green) situations come up more often than most of us realize. Let's look at the following scenario.

> *Luna's grandparents gave her a large sum of money for her twelfth birthday. She wanted to spend the money on stuffed animals and dolls and use whatever was left on new charms for her bracelet. Her mother felt she should put half in a savings account and only spend the other half. How can she use this situation to engender trust as a mother and empower Luna to learn to make the right decisions and trust in herself?*

The mother in this situation has a few options.

1. She can assert her authority (Red/no) and immediately deposit half of the amount in an account before Luna even sees the money. This will not allow Luna to use her own decision-making capabilities and probably will invite tremendous resentment. In the future she might be so averse to thinking responsibly about money that she will spend it indiscriminately, enjoying her newfound freedom and possibly find herself in serious debt.

2. She can immediately tell Luna she can spend whatever she wants as long as it makes her happy. Here too she would encourage her daughter to follow her desires without giving her the chance to consider the benefits of a more cautious attitude toward money. Most likely, in this situation, the long-term results will be similar to those I described above.

3. Or she can maximize the amazingly important benefits of Yellow = Trust = Slow by teaching Luna how to handle money. This financial birthday windfall could be an opportune teaching moment. This can be accomplished by doing the following.

DESCRIBE THE SITUATION

Luna, Grandpa and Grandma sent you this huge amount of money because they think since you're twelve you're capable of deciding how to use it wisely.

Here she describes Luna's competencies as she sees them, even though Luna hasn't thought of herself in this light.

TEACH A LIFE LESSON

Here is an opportunity to teach a life lesson. The mother could say:

> *Usually when we receive such a large amount of money we want to enjoy part of it right away, but also put some away so we know we have saved for the future.*

Luna will remember this during the future stages of her life. Learning a life lesson through an experience which makes it relevant is the best way to make the lesson come alive for our children.

GIVE A CHOICE

> *I want you to think about how much you want to put away and what you really want to spend the rest of the money on, okay?*

Here Luna's mother is laying out a template for responsible money management, but leaving the exact amounts up to Luna. This gives Luna a sense of control and invites her to become part of the solution.

Using these skills would add tremendously to Luna's self-confidence. Not only will she feel better about herself in this situation, but it is safe to guess this experience, and others like it, will help her make wise financial decisions down the road.

ONLY OFFER CHOICES YOU ARE COMFORTABLE WITH

I asked mothers in my GPS group what they thought would happen if despite using the three techniques described above, Luna still refused to take the suggestion and save some of the money. They agreed they would feel challenged if after doing and saying everything "right," their child refused to listen and remained adamant about carrying out her misguided decision. This is where our next Yellow skill comes into play.

When you aren't happy with the choice your child has made, consider whether you offered only choices that were acceptable to you. For example, if you allowed Luna to decide to spend whatever amount she wanted and save the rest and she chose to only save five out of her hundred dollars, would you be okay with that? If so, great! If not, you needed to set some more specific parameters. In a situation like this perhaps you allow her to decide how much she can spend, but you give her a range, such as between twenty-five and sixty dollars. Then, even if she spent sixty, you would still feel good about her choice—and so would she.

Another shortcoming we often fall into is adding "or not" to the end of a question. Often this question isn't really a question at all. For example, "Are you getting on the bus or not?" Every mother knows this isn't really a question. Rather, it's an example of an unfortunate choice of words we use when we are exasperated. We have no intention of allowing them *not* to get on the bus, but we couch our commands in a fake question form nonetheless.

To prevent rejecting your child's choice, only offer them options you are truly okay with, such as the spending range example above. Only then can both you and your child reap the benefits of using this wonderful opportunity and allowing them to grow.

With that in mind, here are a few cautionary alerts:

➢ If you are not okay with your child refusing to help put away the toys, don't give them the choice by asking them if they want to or not. What will you do if he says no?

➢ If you refuse to allow her to continue being friends with the problematic neighbor don't ask her if she thinks she is a good friend to have. What will you do if she says yes?

➢ If you are not okay with Luna spending all her money right now, then don't leave it up to her to decide if she is willing to save some.

The first step necessary before implementing the Yellow light GPS skills is taking an honest look at what you can truly accept when offering your child a choice. Let's see what you come up with.

If you found this more difficult than creating a list of no's as you did in the Red section, don't be surprised. It is much easier for us to know what we don't want and what we won't stand for. It can be a bit difficult to take a step back and allow our children to decide on certain things for themselves and allow them to deal with the consequences.

So the next time you give your child a reasonable choice and she makes a decision she's not so happy with, allow that to be a life lesson for her without worrying about how crushing it might be. Next time she'll remember her prior choice and hopefully make a decision that she is happier with.

CHOOSING THE WORDS YOU REALLY MEAN

Wouldn't it be wonderful if your children listened to every word you said? Do you dream of a time when you won't have to call them, tell them, or warn them a thousand times before they do what you asked them to do? That sounds idyllic doesn't it? Although most mothers complain about their children never listening to them, there are times when they do pay attention to every single word. This is why being accurate with our words is another component in the foundation of creating trust.

Imagine the following common scenario.

It is a lazy Sunday morning. The house is a mess, the kids are cranky, the weather outside is glorious, and you want to . . . be a good mother. When you're not physically at work, (although you may be thinking about an upcoming meeting, a big project, or a particular client you're working with) you want to enjoy the time with your children.

So you say:

> *Kids, if you let me work for an hour on my computer while you pick up the toys in the playroom and straighten out the bookshelves, we can all go to the park. I'll even allow you to take your bikes along this time.*

Sounds like a plan doesn't it? And they agree. They let you work (okay, with interruptions every five minutes, but it is Sunday). But then you get an email from the office that upsets you. In addition, you've recently started a new diet, have gone off carbs and have a raging headache. Over the last half hour the formerly glorious day has been covered by clouds and frankly you're no longer in the mood to go anyplace, let alone with three active children you'll need to keep a close eye on while they zip around on their bikes. So despite your promised plans, you now tell them that you will order in pizza or let them stay up later, you're sorry, but the park is out. You're entitled to a bad day, right? Is it really that terrible to change your plans?

Let's answer these questions by breaking it down. You gave your word to your children and then as a result of how you felt, you changed your plans. What this did was teach your children not to trust you the next time you suggest or promise something. I realize you didn't use the word "promise," but everything you say to a child is internalized as a promise. Let this be a warning to you even when you're innocently thinking out loud.

And yes, we are all entitled to bad days, but as in everything else in life, when we have those difficult moments, we must ask ourselves if whatever we thought to cancel (plans) or do (eat a gallon of rocky-road ice cream) is really to our benefit in the long run.

What can we do instead? How can we navigate the twists and turns of life without losing our children's trust? An important component in accomplishing this is to be precise when saying something. This might sound obvious; after all, you realize the importance of accuracy when building your professional reputation. But think about this, as adults we understand that mitigating circumstances might force us to change a given plan. Sometimes when we say things or other people assure us, it was honest and accurate at that moment, but due to unforeseen circumstances, it might not work out. Children, on the other hand, don't realize this. When we say something, anything, they want to be able to rely on us no matter what happens and know we will follow through. This is the bedrock of a child's trust in us and it fosters their confidence in our ability as parents. It also creates the feeling of family that creates an atmosphere of safety, predictability, and security.

When we aren't careful to follow through, no matter how we feel or what has changed, our children see us as hypocritical or irresponsible—and neither makes it easy for them to rely on us. Being aware of this compels us to be cautious with our words.

Considering the example above when you asked your children to let you work for an hour, anything short of following through exactly as you described will defeat this purpose. If you want to take schedule and mood fluctuations into consideration without damaging your children's faith in you, try this instead.

> *Kids, if you let me work for an hour on my computer while you pick up the toys in the playroom and straighten out the bookshelves, we'll do something fun together. We'll decide what that will be as soon as I finish this report.*

Do you notice the difference between the statements? The second one is vague, but unless you are one hundred percent sure you'll follow through on the plans for riding bikes in the park, don't promise that. The second version not only gives you leeway for possible change, but since you didn't create specific expectations, you have room for negotiation.

By realizing the power of your words and their impact on your relationship with your children, choosing what you say wisely will become second nature to you, if it hasn't already.

BUMPS IN THE ROAD

WHEN YOUR CHILD CANNOT DECIDE

What happens if despite all your good intentions your child can't decide what he or she wants to do? If our objective is to encourage independent thinking and responsibility, the following suggestions can be helpful.

> *Latrice, I hear you telling me you don't know what you want to do. Let's go over the different possibilities and then tell me which of these you don't want to do.*

When we help our children brainstorm, they often find it easier to use the process of elimination, or saying what they don't want to do. This helps narrow down the options and makes it simpler to choose from a smaller list.

Another approach is to ask their opinion by putting it like this:

> *What would you tell a friend if they asked you what to do in a situation like this?*

Sometimes, taking a step back and articulating what kind of advice they would give others helps them clarify what they personally would prefer. Both of the above-mentioned suggestions are also helpful to mothers who encounter difficulties making decisions. When you find yourself at a crossroads, use the process of elimination or ask yourself what you would advise a friend.

KEEP YOUR OPINIONS TO YOURSELF

We usually find ourselves commenting on anything and everything our children do. Many times this can be beneficial, but when creating situations where we want to encourage our children to feel free to make choices and to learn from them, our comments and opinions may actually be counterproductive. For example:

> *Justin, I gave you the choice of lending your video game to your cousin or keeping it to yourself, but I explained to you that if you did lend it you couldn't complain when you wanted to play with it. Since you decided to give it to him, you need to figure out what to do without it.*

Yes, you did give him a choice; to give or not to give. But the GPS way of maximizing your child's capability of learning to make decisions and living with the results is to remain calm and collected when he reacts the way you suspected he might in this circumstance.

Let Justin live with the fact that he made a choice he now regrets. If he sees your impatience as a result of him not making the decision you had hoped he would, he will not trust you when you present him with options the next time around. He will correctly assume that you have your own agenda and don't really trust him to choose the correct option. At the same time, try not to show too much emotion when he makes what you deem as the "correct" choice. If you are careful to express neutral acceptance no matter what your child decides, next time he will be able to base his decision on the natural consequences of his previous choices. This is GPS parenting at its best.

After practicing how to use the assessment skills to facilitate appropriate decisions made by you and your children, we can now move on to earning our children's trust. We earn trust by demonstrating time and again how we have their best interests in mind.

There will be many times when your child will not see things your way, when because of their limited childish view, they are most likely to interpret your caring behavior as being mean or unnecessary. Knowing this, and considering their reactions, will allow you to accept their complaints while remaining calm, confident and being the mother they need you to be. You can explain to them your good intentions using words they can understand. If they can't comprehend at this point, they may look back when they are older and appreciate your insight.

SPEED TACTICS

USE THE WHEN/THEN FORMULA

There will be times when your child will ask to be given more independence. At other times you will feel that your child is ready to begin assuming responsibility for certain chores, choices, or activities. A good way to clarify your expectations and to make sure you are in tune with your child's pace is to use the when /then condition.

> *When you show me you are able to come home on time without me having to remind you, then I will allow you to play outside before doing your homework.*

Instead of forcing him to finish his homework while his friends are playing outside because you don't trust him to come home in time to finish before bedtime, allow him the chance to earn this change in schedule by proving he can come in on his own.

Here's another example:

> **When** you stop fighting with your brothers, **then** I will think about taking you somewhere. I don't enjoy going out with children who can't get along.

As an alternative to threatening to stay at home because you are sick of their constant quarreling, you can phrase it with a when/then condition allowing them to choose what they prefer. When we present options in this manner, children choose the responsible option, which is what your intention was all along.

This Yellow skill is not only helpful when wanting to allow more independence, but is also a wonderful tool to gain cooperation and deal with conflict. Try it and see how these two simple words can change a tense situation into an opportunity for growth.

TRANSFORMING RED SITUATIONS INTO YELLOW ONES

As your children grow older, you will find that many situations, which were a clear no up until a certain stage, can become Yellow maybes. For example:

When my daughter was five I wouldn't let her go to the corner store alone, but now that she is in second grade I will allow it and see how it goes.

I would never have considered allowing him to use real tools when building in the basement, but now that he is older I think he can learn how to handle a hammer and nails with appropriate caution.

By allowing your children to step up and take more responsibility when age appropriate, you are doing what parents should do; adjusting the rules of the road to your children's age and maturity stage. Take it slowly. Try to encourage your child to take more responsibility as you feel they are ready for it, and make sure they earn your trust by showing they are capable and willing to do what is necessary to prove their reliability. A helpful tactic when wanting to encourage this Yellow zone of trusting their capabilities is using the when/then formula.

This is a very exciting and empowering stage in your journey as a parent. After so many years of constant devotion and endless investment, you are finally able to allow your children greater independence to enjoy their newfound capabilities. At this point they should be able to do more for themselves and be excited to be given additional freedom and more responsibility.

PERTINENT YELLOW ROAD SIGNS TO BOOST YOUR PARENTING PROFICIENY

YELLOW SLIPPERY WHEN WET = SLOW DOWN

Have you ever been behind the wheel on a stormy day, barely able to see out the windshield despite your wipers trying to clear a way through the slashing rain? Have you had to drive during a thunderstorm holding tightly to the wheel as you attempt not to slip and slide when pressing the brakes? As you know, these conditions lead to feelings of anxiety and feeling overwhelmed.

Raising children while investing in our careers can lead to similar feelings of being overwhelmed and anxious. This can affect our capabilities to stay safely on course. Just like we need to slow down and use caution while braving the roads in inclement weather, we need to use special skills when parenting during difficult or hectic times.

The Yellow road sign Slippery When Wet in the GPS skill set, alerts us to dangerous road conditions and indicates that caution is necessary. It is up to the driver to decide how to be mindful and exert extra care to prevent dangerous accidents. What follows is the skill set necessary to help us parent our children in similarly treacherous conditions.

THE IMPORTANCE OF SELF-CARE FOR MOMS

The first component of this Slippery When Wet road sign, is the need for us to realize how important it is to slow down and take care of ourselves. When we neglect our physical, emotional, personal, or spiritual needs, we are causing ourselves to run our "engine" on empty. Being caught in a rainstorm with an empty gas tank truly complicates matters. It is up to you to be aware of what you need to be your best, and to make it a priority to do what it takes so that you can function at maximum capacity. Just as rain can cause dangerous conditions on the road, many factors affect the way we are able to parent at any given moment. What exactly am I referring to?

Think about how you respond to small annoyances, such as a child asking you the same question over and over when you are hungry, thirsty, tired, and trying to juggle home and work all while running on empty. What happens when you are affected by the humidity on a long summer day, are feeling sick, or haven't gotten enough exercise and find yourself walking around on autopilot trying to accomplish everything on your never-ending to-do list? Are you able to be patient and understanding? Can you muster up the energy to wisely enforce the Red Rules or even be motivated to take the leap and trust your children to manage more on their own? If you are like most mothers, parenting our children when we are not at our best usually leaves a lot to be desired.

Sherry works full time running the office for an assemblyman and is the mother of twin girls aged seven and a baby. She had this to share:

I didn't realize how exhausted I was until I found myself screaming at my girls when they asked me what time dinner would be served. I am embarrassed to say that a neighbor knocked on the door to see if everything was okay. When she left I sat down and cried for the longest time. My girls were so traumatized to see me out of control that they hid in their room and didn't come out until much later.

That was my wakeup call. I hadn't been sleeping or eating regularly because of a very stressful political campaign, and everyone around me was suffering. Becoming aware of the dangerous road I was traveling on was of major importance for me. It gave me permission to take care of myself. Right now my main motivation is to take better care of my children. I hope that soon I will feel comfortable being kind to myself, because it is the right thing to do...for my own benefit.

I hope you realize that under difficult circumstances it won't be easy to regulate your emotions, responses, and interactions. And that is totally understandable. We are all human. But we need to take responsibility for making sure we are aware of what we need more (or less) of so that we can function both as successful mothers and professionals.

I know that to those reading this book, everyone and everything else is very important, but please note that nobody is as important as you! That's right. You read that correctly. You devote your life to your family and at the same time invest enormous amounts of energy into your profession. Take the following universal truth seriously. Any success you experience with your children or in your career is dependent on how well you are able to carry out your obligations; how well you can fulfill your role. And that depends on how well you treat yourself.

No two people are alike. Only you know what you really need. Some working mothers need more social interaction, others find that they need more time alone. Some mothers invest in more household help, while others prefer the entire family doing chores together, building competence while bonding.

Know yourself. Address your needs. Be proactive in giving yourself what you know you need. You will be doing yourself a favor, but more surprisingly, when your basic physical, social, emotional, and spiritual needs are met, you will be calm and patient, and those who count the most will thank you.

Julie, a physician's assistant and a mother of one son, shared the following.

> I found myself being very sarcastic with my partner and very irritated with my son. I couldn't figure out what it was they were doing to cause this. But after the lesson on the Yellow self-care skill, it hit me. It wasn't anything they were doing that was causing me to behave this way; it was something I wasn't doing!
>
> I was totally neglecting the yoga classes I had attended regularly. I also wasn't eating or sleeping enough due to work stress and a new diet I had recently started. Becoming aware of how mistreating myself was affecting me and those I loved motivated me to

make the necessary changes. I am glad to report that as soon as I got back on track things calmed down considerably. This Yellow road sign was a lifesaver.

THE ART OF RECALIBRATING AND RE-EVALUATING

Struggling with time constraints and hectic schedules, both at home and at work, impacts our ability to be calm and content. Can this reality be changed by extra household help and a good night's sleep? I wish it were that easy. Intense emotions and personal challenges affect us greatly. When you are worried, frustrated, overwhelmed, conflicted, or feeling guilty, your parenting will inevitably be affected. When you are concerned about a work issue or struggling with a financial challenge, what do your children see, hear, and feel? Sherry, one of the mothers I coach privately, shared this very moving story with me.

A few years ago on a hot, humid summer day, she decided to arrange for time off from work to take her children to the park for a picnic dinner. She felt very guilty working all summer while they were out of school and decided to create a memory to treasure by spending quality time together.

She really invested thought and effort in preparing the picnic. She bought a special plaid tablecloth and matching tableware, prepared everyone's favorite foods, and even remembered to pack balls and kites. She researched the best picnic grounds and set off with music playing and a prayer in her heart, hoping that this rare family outing would go well.

She thought of everything (including bringing along Band-Aids and a portable speaker to have music playing while they ate), but there was one thing she couldn't control no matter how much heart and soul she invested in ensuring this would be a wonderful day; the weather!

After just two hours of enjoyable family time, the clouds thickened and thunder rumbled, and she saw her well-laid plans of a wonderful summer day fading fast. She hoped the weather would hold for a bit, but sooner than she could imagine, it started to drizzle and then began raining even harder. Fighting back tears of disappointment she ran around frantically gathering all the stuff to take to the car before everything got soaked. Half-eaten food, soggy board games, soaked napkins, and coloring books, were all thrown on the back seat.

To make matters worse, one of her daughters insisted on jumping on her piggyback style and wouldn't let go. She was aggravated beyond words and angrily shook her daughter off, while screaming that instead of helping she was, as usual, making things harder. Why couldn't she help gather the stuff and run to the car like a normal child?

The trip home was sullen and silent. She was extremely disappointed but was even more upset at herself for snapping at her daughter. All she had wanted was to dedicate this day to creating happy family memories. But then, suddenly, she remembered a GPS guideline suggesting that after a difficult day, interaction, or episode, it's best to give the benefit of the doubt and then press restart and begin again. At times, as when driving on a slippery road, you might have to slow down and pull over before continuing on your journey.

That night when she tucked her daughter in, by using her Yellow GPS skills, Sherry gave her daughter the benefit of the doubt and asked her what she was thinking when she kept jumping on her back, despite seeing that her mother was rushing around like a madwoman trying to beat the rain. And do you know what her daughter told her? "Mommy, I saw how hard you worked to give us all a good time and then it started raining and I saw you hadn't brought an umbrella so I wanted to cover you so it would rain on me and not on you."

Wow. Touching! Childish and clumsy, but oh so moving. Imagine if Sherry hadn't asked for an explanation and had made do with the natural assumption that her daughter was just being impossible. This very emotional moment would have been lost forever. So, don't jump to conclusions. Ask. Be curious. View the world from your child's perspective. You never know what you will learn.

SPEAK UP OR BE SILENT?

As powerful as words are, sometimes the power of silence is even greater. Over the years we have used words to convey, connect, and create change. You have discovered how to use words with your loved ones at home and with your colleagues in the workplace. Hopefully by now you feel more comfortable and competent when communicating. So now it's time to explore the power of silence.

Keeping quiet, not using words, is much more difficult than expressing our thoughts and feelings. When we are faced with situations that demand silence or restraint, we need to overcome our driving need to be heard, our instinctive pull to respond. As a mother it is even more difficult, because we feel that sharing our thoughts and needs with our children is important and helps them understand us, our needs, wants and reasons for doing or not doing what they requested of us.

The Yellow, Slippery When Wet, road sign is there to remind us to slow down and ask ourselves, "Is now really the best time to say what is on the tip of my tongue? Will it serve me and my children well if I speak without thinking?" What is usually needed is a moment of caution to reflect upon whether your instant reaction, if communicated, will make things better, or more likely, worse. Knowing when to talk and when not to, is true power. Why not say exactly what you think when you feel you should? How do we know when to be silent and when to speak? Take a look at the examples below:

> *I want my daughter to know in no uncertain terms exactly what I won't tolerate!*

> *I want my son to realize that he can't do whatever he wants whenever he wants! He doesn't pay the mortgage around here!*

Sound familiar? Do you want to express yourself like this at times? The following is a sampling of what other mothers participating in the online GPS program and in my coaching groups suggested when sharing what they thought defined slippery roads in their parenting journey. They suggested you think before you speak in the following situations:

➢ If you are in a rush.
➢ If your child is in a rush, such as halfway out the door to practice, school, or errands.
➢ If there are other people around.
➢ If you are just venting and haven't clarified your message.
➢ If you know what you are about to say will create escalation and be counterproductive.
➢ If it will invite the immediate resistance of your partner.
➢ If it is a larger issue that will not be resolved by what you want to say and needs more serious attention.
➢ When you are too angry to be coherent.
➢ When your children are too angry to be able to listen.

I am sure you can add more to this list. If you want to choose what is most pertinent to your situation, ask yourself... how angry, rushed, or coherent am I? How will she react if you tell her this? What might his reaction be when he hears what you are thinking right now? How will communicating when you feel like this affect your relationship? Is there anyone around that might overhear your dialogue which will unnecessarily escalate the issue?

Something important to keep in mind (don't we all know this), is that once we say something it is very difficult, if not impossible, to undo the great impact our words have on those around us.

On one hand, this is very heartening because it accords tremendous power to each of our words. When we choose words wisely and convey them with love and conviction, they can create indelible memories.

On the other hand, words spoken indiscriminately with little thought to our tone or message, can harm relationships more than we ever imagined. And that is never our intention. Knowing when to keep silent allows us to maximize the times we do decide to communicate.

We keep quiet to reduce damage and minimize hurt feelings. Silence can also be very restful. When you are in a room with others, each one busy doing their stuff (they are doing homework or reading and you are folding laundry, or looking over your emails) silence can indicate a level of contentment and comfort, giving space and creating a calm haven. Have you experienced this lately? Or are you constantly surrounded by noise and electronic devices on the highest volume? Maybe give blessed silence a try once in a while and savor the difference.

Invoking your Yellow Skills and choosing to remain silent, can often prevent more problems than speaking. Having said that, keep in mind that when silence is used as a weapon (whether it is to intentionally ignore someone or to play deaf to requests for help or attention) it is self-understood that this is abusing the concept of positive silence. Also realize that a lack of response in the face of unacceptable behavior is usually interpreted as condoning the behavior. So just as it is beneficial to think before you speak, it is just as important to understand exactly what your silence is communicating.

Using words and silence wisely, will go far in helping you navigate the slippery journey of parenting.

I remember a time over twenty years ago when, without warning, I lost my voice. That's right: I, the lecturer with a busy private practice, couldn't utter even one word. I had been suffering from a cold for a few days, but nothing had prepared me for the loss of my voice.

I tried to coax a few words out, forcing my vocal chords to produce, but to no avail. Imagine having to get a houseful of children out the door in the morning in no time and with zero speech! (Side note, don't try it). But that's exactly what I did. I walked over to each child and shook them gently awake while pointing to my throat and hoping they wouldn't take advantage of my frustrating limitations. I used my hands and facial expressions to convey what I needed them to do.

I improvised by using body language, a pad and pen, (and wrote in capital letters when I was "silently screaming") and managed to continue my daily schedule during those few days without being able to utter a word.

It was dramatic and to be honest, traumatic. I never realized how much I relied on verbal instructions and actual words. For those few days when words weren't an option, I needed to connect and get my messages across to my children in other ways. It wasn't easy for any of us.

I still remember that frustratingly silent week many decades later. I also remember that for those few days there was hardly any arguing, almost no raised voices, and zero disrespect. Somehow everything got done. This thought made me stop in my tracks and reevaluate the necessity of my constantly using so many words. Since then I haven't been mindful enough about what I say and how I say it, but I do take pride in the fact that those days taught me the value of silence.

BUMPS IN THE ROAD

FEELING SELFISH WHEN MAKING SELF-CARE A PRIORITY

Keep in mind that if you are not taking care of yourself, such as ample sleep and exercise, eating well, and keeping stress to a minimum, your responses to your children's comments most likely will be unfocused and emotionally lacking. Most working mothers feel guilty or selfish when they consider making self-care a priority in their lives. Look at it this way, would you feel guilty for taking your car in for oil changes and routine maintenance? Do you feel guilty when you have to change your tires because they're worn? Of course not. As a working mother, your maintenance is just as important as your vehicle's—even more so I think. Taking care of you allows you to better care for your children and be there for them, physically, emotionally, and spiritually.

If you're struggling with adding self-care activities to your schedule, I recommend starting small. Here are some suggestions.

- ➤ Book a simple coffee date with yourself for thirty minutes.
- ➤ Start going for a walk in the evenings by yourself.
- ➤ Have a relaxing bath once a week after the kids are in bed.

Don't go from zero to sixty miles an hour at once, work your way up. You'll overcome your feelings of selfishness when you realize all the positive benefits of these small self-care activities.

THE TENDENCY TO COMPARE

After discussing the importance of the art of silence, it is fitting to add an important issue pertaining to what we sometimes tell our children.

As mothers we motivate our children to be the best they can be. As working mothers we need to condense this motivation into the precious few hours we have to spend with our children. We do this by providing them with the most enriching education, varied after school activities, and frequent pep talks describing their promising future.

All this is very understandable, even admirable. But all too often, when doing this we compare a child to a sibling, neighbor, friend, or fantasy child. If you were to record your dialogue with your children, would it sometimes sound like this?

> *Why does your room always look like a tornado hit? Why can't you learn from your sister how to keep a room neat and clean?*

> *Why does Todd always do his mother's shopping for her? Every time I ask you to run to the corner store for something you put on a whole song and dance. How did his mother get so lucky?*

You might not categorize such talk as negative, Red GPS talk, but would you agree it does belong in the Yellow Caution Slippery Zone? What might your son or daughter think or feel when they hear you comparing them to others?

Mom doesn't ever notice what I accomplish. My sister never babysits or helps in the kitchen, but all I hear about is how neat her room is. I hate her!

Or

Mom doesn't realize that Todd loves shopping because he always buys stuff for himself without his mom knowing. He is far from being an angel. But I have to bring back the receipt for everything, so it doesn't pay for me to do the shopping.

Did the daughter in the first example feel appreciated for what she **did** contribute to the family? Obviously not. Did she learn any practical skills on how to keep her room neat? It doesn't seem likely. What exactly was accomplished with this interaction besides making her more resistant to offer help in the future and creating a strong dislike for her sister?

In the second example, the only obvious fact is if you can get away with hiding stuff, adults will think you are great. Todd's mother (and her friends) weren't aware of his personal shopping sprees, and therefore held him up as a shining example to his less eager friends who couldn't treat themselves every time they went to the store. Surely that wasn't the confusing message his mother wanted him to internalize when she compared him to Todd.

You are now more aware of the detrimental effects comparisons have on our children and on their self-esteem. The next time you feel yourself slipping into the all too familiar litany of comparisons, ask yourself, "How can I use the Yellow caution sign to help make the right choice on this very slippery road to parenting success?"

It might take time to understand, appreciate, and implement the exciting menu of Yellow skills. Give yourself the time you need. Process is paramount. You will notice yourself becoming aware of these "in between situations" and will discover the magic in using these Yellow skills to create trust and confidence.

SPEED TACTICS

USE SLOW TALK

Since that difficult time when I lost my voice for a while and noticed the benefits of not speaking, I consciously try to take time, slow down, and think before saying something or instinctively responding. I count to five, or sometimes even ten, before answering a question or sharing my opinion about what others are saying or doing. And I have found there is magic in those silent seconds, the place I call the safe zone.

Mom, can I go outside to play even though I didn't do my homework yet... (Me being silent) ... *Forget it!*

*Maybe it's best I finish it now so that I can have more
fun playing outside knowing it's done already.
Maaaaaa..... he's killing me!!! He is grabbing my game
away!* (Me being silent for a moment) ....*Never mind,
the truth is I'm tired of playing so he can have this silly
game anyway.*

Do you see what happened? Before my painful experience of enforced silence, I would jump in with suggestions, rules, regulations, warnings, and peace-keeping efforts. But after seeing the positive results of my being compelled to keep quiet, I create this safe zone by biting my lips and instead give my children the opportunity to fill my silence with their ideas and decisions.

Do they always say or do what I had hoped they would? Of course not. But no matter what the final outcome is, my giving them the gift of silence, of calm acceptance, of another moment to think and reconsider, always has a positive effect and prevents our slipping into even more problematic situations. Truly, proof that less is more.

CREATE A PERSONAL WISH LIST

This is when you should start writing your own personal wish list. See how many ideas you can come up with for activities you would find meaningful, enjoyable or relaxing. Ask yourself what you would do if you had an entire week off at your disposal, with no obligations or responsibilities? How would you spend your time? What would make you happy? You might want to Google self-care suggestions. You will be surprised at how many options are available which don't cost much time or money.

Be adventurous. Try something new as often as possible. Make sure to incorporate fun things to experience as often as you can. By doing so you will not only prevent inevitable burnout, but you will be modeling healthy behavior for your children to emulate.

YELLOW INTERSECTION AHEAD = PREPARING FOR TRANSITIONS

Are any of your days the same? Can you count on things usually working out the way you want and need them to? Most working mothers struggle and constantly juggle changing schedules as well as a rollercoaster of emotions on a daily basis. Does this sound familiar?

Life is a kaleidoscope of change. Things are always happening in flux and changing, then once you get used to the new reality, they change again. The famous quote by Heraclitus, "The only thing that is constant is change," can accurately describe any day in the hectic life of a working mother. As working moms, how do we manage the stress and strain of change while gaining the trust of our children? How can we do things differently, despite the rollercoaster ride of our busy lives, so our children learn to trust us, and also trust themselves?

This Yellow road sign of Intersection Ahead symbolizes the importance of alerting our children to any upcoming changes and helps them prepare for the inevitable transitions in their lives. Imagine yourself in your car seeing that yellow warning sign before reaching an intersection down the road.

What decisions and actions do you take once you are aware of the approaching intersection?

SURVEYING THE ROAD AHEAD AS A FAMILY

This Yellow = Slow Intersection Ahead road sign adds significantly to the working mother's GPS skill set. It prepares us as parents to help our children navigate the many necessary changes which affect them on a daily basis.

Can you think of any important upcoming transitions that will impact your child's life? Are you surprised at what you came up with? Many mothers in the GPS groups have shared common transitions their children face such as: a new sibling being born, moving to a different home or city, starting first grade or high school, parents divorcing, going away to college, and a mother starting a job when she was previously a homemaker.

These situations, and many more, are all part of the fascinating tapestries that make up our lives. From an adult's perspective we may see them as integral and necessary parts of life. Often, what we don't realize is how children can feel shocked, afraid, and even traumatized by things we have learned to take in stride.

Most of the above-mentioned transitions usually come about as a result of choices parents have made. This means that we, as mothers, have had ample time to contemplate and accept these changes, whereas our children have not been privy to this process. We knew, we chose, and we decided. They didn't. And this is not the only issue. Despite the constant focus on the importance of choice and the advantages of variety, most people do not like change and some are simply paralyzed by the thought of it.

Even when we are simply a bit uncomfortable or unhappy, most times we elect to remain in our seats, our jobs, or our relationships rather than invest the energy needed and take the risk inherent in choosing to change. With so much natural resistance to change, it is even more important for us to pave the way so that our children will learn how to cope with change in the best possible manner.

By preparing children in advance, we are giving them the opportunity they need to come to terms with the new reality. Even if the change is for the best, children usually have a very one-dimensional perspective about life, which I have come to call, "What's In It for Me?" or WIIFM. A new sibling or a new school will certainly make a child's life less convenient and you can confidently predict they will not be thrilled. How can we help children prepare for upcoming transitions?

BE AN ACTIVE LISTENER

When preparing our children for upcoming changes, give them as much information as possible to make them feel comfortable with the change. Also, devote enough time and have the patience to hear how they feel and think about it. None of us likes to be told that our lives will be impacted without being given the opportunity to express our thoughts, fears, and needs. The first step to helping a child prepare his or herself is to learn the three parts that comprise the skill of attentive listening.

First: ask your child to talk about all the things they are worried or upset about regarding a particular change. Second: listen, really listen. Don't try to convince or explain. No need to share the logic of why this new situation was necessary. Third: repeat back to your child the difficulties your child is expressing.

This is not the time to explain why the change must occur or convince your child it is for the best. This is the time to truly listen to your child and hear their concerns and fears. Explaining and sharing reasons behind the necessity for the change can come later. For example, you might say to your daughter:

> I hear how scared you are to walk into a new school when you don't know anybody there. That's not easy!

> I know you are upset because when we move we will not have a backyard and we will be in an apartment instead of a house. I can understand that.

If at this moment you don't have time for these three parts of attentive listening, you can offer to discuss the matter later. Make a "date" for when it's convenient, so your child is assured you will make time to truly listen.

TAKING THE EMOTIONAL HIGH ROAD

Remember that you are always in the driver's seat. No child and no situation can **make** you angry, nervous, or out of control. As farfetched as it might seem to you now, how we feel and how we respond is our choice. You can learn to take the high road and know your reactions and responses will ensure you reach the goal you have set for yourself as a mother. This will not only be a priceless gift of love to your family, it will give you many reasons to be proud of yourself and enable you to better succeed in your career.

How can your child know what to expect of you? How can he predict what you will say or do? The answer to that is conditional. When mothers aren't aware of the importance emotional consistency plays in creating trust, they usually don't give much thought to their mood fluctuations. But when viewed from a child's perspective, especially through the lens of credibility, the benefit of regulating our emotions becomes glaringly clear.

When you consistently use the Yellow = Trust = Slow GPS factor in raising your children, they will learn they can rely on you to prepare them for any and all changes in their lives. This in turn gives them the confidence that they are safely buckled in next to you and you are in the driver's seat with your hands firmly on the steering wheel. Since children are convinced that the world revolves around them, by describing your emotional state they will be relieved to hear that it isn't because of them. It's difficult enough for children to deal with us (adults) when we are tired, upset, emotionally drained, or frustrated without the added burden of assuming that all this is somehow their fault.

By preparing your children ahead of time, you are creating trust and allowing them to adjust to the new idea, the changed situation, and the upcoming challenge. When they are not caught off guard, they can more easily deal with the situation.

Knowing they can trust you to prepare them for upcoming situations helps them feel calm and confident. When they grow older and face important transitions in their lives they will be able to cope with those changes with confidence, because you trained them to be aware of and how to deal with the inevitable changes in life. This in turn will encourage them to prepare those around them when they foresee changes on the horizon.

FOSTERING TRUST BY BEING EMOTIONALLY PREDICTABLE

Something we don't often pay enough attention to is how our mood fluctuations affect our relationships with our children, which in turn impacts their ability to trust us. When discussing the importance of a Yellow warning road sign indicating changes ahead, it is obvious that if we cultivate stability we will be setting the stage for raising secure confident children. This not only means having consistent, predictable routines, but it also encompasses being emotionally predictable.

Imagine a child coming home to a mother who is singing and lovingly affectionate (you finally got that promotion) and the next day she is a quiet, withdrawn mother who hardly utters one-word sentences (your colleague got that promotion). Or, you are usually very expressive and excited when your daughter receives good grades on her report card, even calling Grandma to share the news, but this time you are distracted and hardly glance at her hard-earned grades. Do you consistently show interest in who his close friends are, but lately don't pay attention even when he shares the worrisome descriptions of what they have been up to?

If your moods fluctuate, as in the examples above, how can your child know what to expect of you? How can he predict your usual reactions? The answer is, most of the time he can't. When mothers aren't aware of the importance emotional consistency plays in creating trust, they usually don't give a thought to their emotional fluctuations. But when viewed from a child's perspective, especially through the lens of creating trust, the benefit of regulating our emotions becomes glaringly obvious.

The following is a possible scenario played out in two different ways.

Twelve-year-old Nia is talking to her friend:

> *Lilly, I can't ditch school and play hooky. My mom will freak out and it's not worth it!*

Nia's statement is an obvious outcome of a clear value system imparted by a mother who is emotionally predictable. When your child is certain about your reaction, when you are consistently predictable, they can make decisions, some of them life-changing, based on what they know you will feel, say, or do.

When a mother is not at all predictable in her responses, her values, or her reactions, the following dialogue might transpire instead.

Lilly, great idea! Let's ditch social studies and meet in the park. My mom will probably be okay with it even if she finds out... if I catch her in a good mood!

This is the difference between a child who can predict your responses and a child who is taking advantage of her mother's unpredictable reactions. Try this short exercise: list five situations that might arise with your children and describe your predictable reactions to the situations. What did you notice while reviewing the situations you listed?

If you found this task difficult, you are not alone. It isn't easy to regulate our emotions and reactions, especially when we feel pulled in so many directions while trying to succeed at work and perfect our parenting skills in the few hours we have to spend with our children. Hopefully I have convinced you of the importance of trying to be consistently predictable as often as possible. The following insights might help you manage your emotions and your reactions in a more consistent manner.

Sometimes it is more difficult to regulate emotions due to the following:

External Influences

When you are hungry, thirsty, tired, cold, hot, sick, or don't get enough sleep, exercise, or fresh air, understand that you will find it harder to regulate your emotions. Take responsibility for making sure you give your body what it needs to be able to be able to function as it should. There aren't enough hours in the day to accomplish what we need to do at work as well as at home, but by ignoring your basic needs you are undermining your success. It is not worth it.

Which external situations affect us and force us to slow down, take stock, maybe even change course? It may be that you notice your child isn't doing well and you feel that a change in your schedule would do much to improve that. You may find yourself too tired, overweight or suffering from headaches or backaches more than you would like. Or it could be that it's time for the personal "tune up" every vehicle needs in order to operate optimally on the road. Be aware that external circumstances, whether medical, personal, financial, or environmental, usually greatly impact our feelings and behaviors.

Internal Influences

When you are worried, frustrated, overwhelmed, conflicted, or feeling guilty about the hours you need to be out of the house, you obviously will be emotionally drained. Your responsibility to yourself as a person, and to your children as their mother, is to make sure you have a plan on how best to deal with this. Coping with emotional burnout can take many forms. You can either find somebody you can speak to, arrange for more household help, or initiate much-needed recreation that you have postponed for too long.

Once you find a coping mechanism that works, you will be more in control of yourself and your responses. This will allow you to enjoy your time with your children, while gifting them a mother who, most of the time, is wonderfully predictable in her reactions to their behavior.

It is also important to note that not only is it vital to prepare our children for technical and family transitions, but when we are going through emotional upheavals as well, it is prudent to share these too.

> *Matt, I am under a lot of pressure this week because I am opening the new store. I will be out a lot and when I am home I might be very tired or preoccupied. I want you to know that this has nothing to do with you. I love you very much and as soon as I have everything up and running I will be home by 4:00 pm as usual. I will be less tired once the new store is running smoothly and I will be able to help with homework and read you a nighttime story again. Do you want to talk about this?*

Or

> *Iris, because Grandma is very sick I will be away many nights taking shifts at the hospital. I might also be worried or sad because I love her very much and it is difficult for me to see her suffer like this. Can you understand that?*

Here you are preparing your child not only for a schedule change, but for an emotional intersection. Not all life changes create noticeable emotional fluctuations. When you know they will, the best thing to do is to share this with your children as part and parcel of the upcoming change. Do you realize why this is of major importance when trying to maximize the Yellow/trust component? One of the behaviors that invites trust is emotional consistency. True, we are not robots and children should expect shifting moods. But when we are certain that we will be out of sorts, it is helpful and considerate to let those around us know about the impending emotional detour.

EMBRACING THE LANGUAGE OF RESPONSIBILITY

In order to create and invite trust, we need to be responsible, which means, among other things, to say what you mean and to follow through on commitments.

Often in the course of our lives, we think we will be okay doing something. We institute routines or agree to accommodate someone in need. Then circumstances or moods change and we fail to live up to our obligations. When we are remiss in this, we create confusion and anxiety in those around us. As mentioned, an important component in earning trust is making sure we take our responsibilities seriously. But we also want to raise our children to behave in ways that invite trust.

What can we do when we notice our children being lax with their commitments? How can we raise our children to be more responsible, so they can earn the trust of those around them? Using the language of responsibility is simple, powerful, and very effective. It means using the "wh" questions (who, what, when, and where) to help your child realize what they are (or aren't) doing, thereby emphasizing the need for them to make different choices and change their behavior. The following will shed light on how this skill is used.

The next time you see your child shirking their chores or backing out of a commitment, use these questions and the language of responsibility to make them aware of what they are doing. Then, ask them what they should be doing instead.

If Benjamin is playing instead of doing his homework, you can ask:

> **What** time is it now? (6:30 pm) **What** are you doing? (playing video games). **When** did we agree was the cutoff time for finishing homework? (6:00 pm). Okay, so unless you have no homework, **what** do you think you should be doing right this minute instead of playing?

Here you were able to use neutral "wh" questions to allow Benjamin to realize he was wasting time that was earmarked for homework. Here is another example.

If Violet isn't brushing her teeth regularly, you may ask:

> **Which** toothbrush is yours? (the pink one). **When** was the last time you used it? (I can't remember). **What** did the dentist say about brushing teeth when we saw him last week? (I can prevent cavities by brushing daily). **When** should you be using your toothbrush? (at least once a day). **What** kind of plan can you come up with to help you remember to do this every evening? (uh... not sure but will go up and brush my teeth now).

By using the "wh" questions you are avoiding painful criticism and instead asking questions to help your child realize what it is they are doing and what they should be doing instead. Be aware that it's best not to use a "why" question. Although "why" is considered part of the "wh" question group, it usually sounds accusatory instead of investigative. It might cause defensive or resistant responses, instead of enabling your child to notice what they are doing.

Monica, a mother of four and a psychotherapist in private practice, shared this:

> Sometimes it seems as if I am raising two different families. My two oldest are serious, mature, responsible, and helpful. My two youngest are the exact opposite. I hated myself every time I would scream or threaten the little ones about their behavior. I also didn't want to constantly be policing them. I was concerned they would never learn to behave on their own, but I didn't know what else to do every time they behaved irresponsibly.
>
> After hearing about the language of responsibility in the GPS group, I figured I had nothing to lose. It felt awkward at first; they didn't understand why I was asking them so many questions. But I didn't give up. After a week I noticed when I used the "wh" questions they would invariably understand what they were doing and what they should be doing instead. It was magical to watch them become more responsible.

Using this language creates awareness, which then encourages responsibility. You can begin by using this technique on yourself. Next time you find yourself procrastinating or ignoring your commitments, ask yourself what it is that you are doing and what you know you should be doing instead. See how this works. Then start using this Yellow GPS skill with your children. Not only is it important for them to be able to trust you, but it is vital that they learn from an early age to take their responsibilities seriously. Using this language will help both of you earn trust easily.

BUMPS IN THE ROAD

WHEN UNEXPECTED TRANSITIONS OCCUR

Although we now understand the importance of heeding the Yellow warning sign of Intersection Ahead and preparing our children for upcoming changes in their lives, despite our best intentions there will be times unexpected transitions will occur. Perhaps your toddler's childcare center is closing or your nine-year-old's favorite teacher is moving cross-country in the middle of the year. Maybe you were promoted and need to travel extensively or your spouse is dealing with an unexpected illness. These are all situations out of our control which cannot be planned for in advance.

So how can we help our children cope with these unexpected, upsetting bumps in the road? The first thing is to be aware that we weren't given advance notice so we couldn't prepare them in advance. This realization on its own will allow us to be more sensitive and accepting when they react or respond with annoyance, sadness, or frustration.

When we understand the difficulty of dealing with a change without adequate preparation, we can make ourselves available to listen and connect to their overwhelming feelings and concerns. Sometimes just listening, without judging or sermonizing, is helpful and supportive.

Once your child feels understood and validated, you can try to reframe the unexpected situation as something new and exciting, instead of shocking or disappointing. Situations like these can always be used to practice flexibility, creativity, and problem-solving skills. Children are usually influenced by the perspective expressed by the adults around them. This is your chance to help them see such situations in a more positive light. When we do this, our children will have us as their external compass which will allow them to cultivate an attitude of curiosity and adventure, instead of bitterness and defeat. Being aware of this prevalent bump and preparing ourselves for the unexpected, will create a feeling of confidence and calmness as we parent our children along their road to success.

ALLOWING OUR DIFFICULTY AS PARENTS TO IMPACT OUR CHILDREN

Sometimes in our zeal to prepare our children ahead of time for any and all changes they might encounter, we overlook the necessity to devote enough time to prepare ourselves. When we are overworked and focused on making the lives of those around us easier, we tend to ignore our needs. Often when this happens, we find ourselves responding to upcoming transitions with irritation or resistance. This Yellow bump comes as a surprise to many working moms, because we usually consider ourselves proactive and prepared. But when we don't take the time to share our fears and concerns with a trusted friend, life coach or partner, our children are usually the ones who are most affected by our negative attitude. Giving ourselves the time, support, and validation necessary to be able to deal with the upcoming transitions calmly, is not only a gift to ourselves, but will benefit our children as well.

SPEED TACTICS

INVITE YOUR CHILDREN TO BE PART OF THE SOLUTION

Now is the time to go back to what your child shared when you were listening to their worries and concerns. Choose to focus on something they shared and ask them what they think can be done to make that particular issue less upsetting. You can use the word we, but keep in mind that the goal here is to encourage them to find their own coping strategies to life's many challenges. By doing so, you are not only building their trust in you, but also fostering self-confidence, which is invaluable in life. Take a look at these examples:

What do you think we can do to make it less scary for you to start at a new school?

What can we do so that you won't feel so upset about us not having a back yard?

Don't be surprised or disappointed if your child says, "I don't know." That is to be expected. You can then start by suggesting something, but if you see they aren't in the mood to cooperate brainstorming positives or solutions at that moment, postpone this discussion to a more opportune time. Even if you need to revisit this practical suggestion when you are already in the new situation, it will always be helpful. By knowing how to use this skill you will feel competent to help your children be better prepared, no matter when you use it.

ENGAGE IN COMPETITIVE BRAINSTORMING

After listening to your child's feelings and concerns, I propose you take turns suggesting any good and happy things that might result from the new reality. Try to make this a competitive game since at such times children are resistant to seeing anything positive pertaining to the new reality. A fun game can entice them to cooperate. You can make it easier by being the first one to start by offering a suggestion. Consider promising a prize to the "winner" who comes up with the most creative suggestions (always make sure your child wins, that way you do too). This game has proven most effective in helping children create a positive attitude toward upcoming transitions, despite their prevalent misgivings. For example:

> *True! A new school means nobody remembers anything that happened last year and you can start fresh. It also means that none of the teachers have taught your older brother, so they can't compare you to him.*

You are right. We will be in the city, not in the suburbs, and you will be able to go to the mall and the museum more often because they will be closer. I didn't even think about that!

By inviting their input and showing interest, excitement, and willingness to collaborate with their suggestions and ideas, you are creating the foundations of loving cooperation, fostering independent thinking, and creative problem-solving skills; GPS parenting at its best.

YELLOW GPS SKILLS Q&A REAL QUESTIONS FROM WORKING MOMS JUST LIKE YOU

I feel more confident with the clear Red skills. What can I do to become more comfortable in the Yellow zone?

This is a very common question raised in my parenting groups. For most working mothers the parenting comfort zone is either in the Red (saying no) or in the Green (saying yes). It takes more time and thought to understand and use the Yellow (caution) skill set. Once you are clear about how useful the Yellow assessment/decision skills are and you start using the tips and suggestions, you will be able to widen your menu of choices as a parent. By practicing the clear, actionable tips and tactics described above, you will gain confidence and competence using the Yellow skill set. This will not only allow you and your children to develop and mature as they emulate decision-making skills, but you will also enjoy using these effective methods in the work place.

Why do you say that comparisons are negative when they can also motivate children?

Some people think children feel motivated when compared to peers or siblings who are better or brighter than they are. But in all the years I have been working with families, I haven't seen that to be the case. If anything, much of my practice has entailed mitigating the damage done to children whose main method of motivation was using comparisons. A better motivator would be to paint a picture of how your child could shine if they made wiser choices and learned new skills. Compare your son to what you envision him being in the future, creating a positive and realistic goal and expressing assurance that he has the wherewithal to actualize that vision.

Describe to your daughter how things could be if she would invest the time and the effort to develop her unique innate talents. Being compared to their shining future selves will be an inspiring motivator. It is definitely much less damaging than having you compare them to others because they fall short.

What can I do if despite all my efforts I can't seem to control my mood fluctuations?

I assume you are asking this after making every effort to incorporate the suggestions given earlier concerning this issue. If despite everything you've attempted you are still struggling, realize that you are dealing with intense emotions which are difficult to regulate. This may be due to unresolved childhood experiences, difficulty juggling parenting and work, or complications dealing with other aspects of your life. In such a case, you might seriously consider contacting a professional to help shine a light on what is bothering you and to help you internalize and implement proven methods which can greatly enhance your peace of mind. This might even be a blessing in disguise. By realizing the importance of stabilizing your emotions for the sake of your children, you too will benefit. Once you have the support, direction and inspiration you need, you will see tremendous improvement in your parenting and in your personal happiness.

By now you should feel comfortable using all the GPS skills at your disposal to raise happy children while investing in your career. This Yellow Intersection Ahead road sign is symbolic of all the wonderful changes and life transitions awaiting your children on their roads to adulthood. Use the wide array of Yellow GPS skills to allow them greater freedom, to delegate age-appropriate responsibility, and to enable their growing independence as they start out on their unique journeys to success in life.

You have now completed the third part of the parenting skill sets contained in this book. You have clarified and internalized what the concept of parenting with trust is and by now can recognize how the universal Yellow traffic signal and road signs symbolize vital life-changing parenting skills. These skills will add much to your competence, both with your children, and in the workplace.

IMPLEMENTING YOUR YELLOW SKILLS LIKE A PRO IN THE WORKPLACE

APPLYING YELLOW LIGHT TACTICS AT WORK TO FOSTER AN ATMOSPHERE OF COMPETENCY

Now that you understand, have internalized, and successfully implemented many of the GPS Yellow skills with your children, it is time to utilize them in your work environment. The Yellow = Trust = Slow components are vital in order to delegate and create an atmosphere of competency. By using these effective skills, you can earn the trust of those you work with while enabling them to believe in themselves.

Nellie, a mother of two and the director of a large real estate company, shared this:

> Our firm was growing by leaps and bounds because the real estate market was hot. I hired many new brokers, but still found myself swamped with work. I couldn't understand why, although my payroll was growing weekly, I was working longer hours than ever.

After coming home from a GPS group, I discussed the Yellow skill set with my husband. He pointed out that instead of encouraging the new brokers and delegating responsibilities, I micromanaged their every move and created even more stress for myself.

I found it liberating to implement the Yellow GPS skills that allowed the new recruits to take important clients to house showings and preside over complex closings. I couldn't believe how well they did on their own and how relieved I was. There were some glitches, but nothing that couldn't be rectified. The confidence they gained by being allowed the professional experience served my firm well. Had I not utilized the GPS skills at that point I am sure I would still be hovering over them and by now would be burned out with few sales and no personal time to enjoy with my family. I never would have imagined how learning to use successful parenting skills would lead to professional accomplishment, but it does.

What leadership qualities inherent in the Yellow skill set do you need to demonstrate at work to earn the gift of trust? As with parenting, being accurate in what you say and commit to is of major importance. When your employees and bosses know they can rely on you to follow through with whatever you took upon yourself, they will trust you. Keep in mind that every word you utter will be put under a magnifying glass and repeated back to you when you least expect it. Conversations overheard in the coffee room validate this.

She promised to let us know if they were going through with the merger and I believe her. She has yet to let me down.

She asked me to take over her shift today and agreed to take mine on Thanksgiving. Although November is four months away, I have no problem relying on her commitment. She always follows through.

BE CONSISTENT IN EMOTIONS AND REACTIONS

Another important factor which engenders trust is consistency in your emotions and reactions. How would you feel if sometimes your boss was oblivious to you staying many hours overtime and at other times held you up as the employee of the month to be emulated by everyone. Never knowing if your dedication would be ignored or rewarded would be frustrating and unnerving, wouldn't you agree? Or how would you feel if your long-time employee had extreme mood swings and you never knew if the calm happy secretary or the impatient rude one was showing up that day? Inconsistency and inaccuracy breed distrust. Meaning what you say, following through no matter how difficult, and being consistent with your emotions and interactions engender trust.

Just like when you are on the road and you slow down when you approach a yellow signal, there are times at work when it is necessary to proceed with caution. Sometimes you need to make an important decision which will affect the entire workplace. At other times you need to take action that will impact a specific client or employee. How can you consistently make wise decisions under the very stressful conditions found in most professional environments?

Making the right decisions is a great responsibility, especially at work where they impact clients, co-workers and the financial health of your business. This chapter is not an in-depth analysis of the best ways to reach crucial, necessary decisions, but the Yellow skill set does clarify how to maximize the choices you make so you can create an atmosphere of trust, confidence, and cooperation.

EMPLOY THE THREE QUESTIONS OF COLLABORATION

You might be the boss, the supervisor, or the department head. Perhaps this business was your brainchild and you have invested your heart and soul into making it the success it is today. Or maybe you are the most experienced employee in your department due to the many years you've worked there. Whatever the situation might be, and despite the fact that you really might know best how things could and should be done, the magic word in any workplace is collaboration.

Whether between management, the work force, the decision makers, those out in the field, or even between you and your clients, when there is trust, cooperation, and collaboration everyone feels connected and invested in doing their best to achieve success. What is a simple proven way to accomplish this? By using the three common "wh" questions: who what and which.

Who is involved and whom will it effect?

What are my options now?

Which option is the safest (personally, emotionally, financially, etc.) for all those concerned in this specific situation?

Randi, a mother of two and a trauma specialist who works nights in the emergency room, shared the following.

After using GPS successfully with my children, I brought it to the attention of the HR department in my hospital. They agreed to have the entire ER medical staff take a crash course in the GPS method with the focus on implementing those skills in the workplace. It is gratifying to see how after a few months we are all using the same skill set and language.

For example, last night a very disturbed patient was creating havoc in the waiting room. It was magical to see how the attending nurses and doctors used the "wh" questions to resolve the situation. They asked the patient who could be called to come and stay with him so that he would feel safe while waiting. They enquired as to what his chief issues were so that they could alert client services. They clarified which medications he was on. Within two minutes, by using the GPS Yellow skills, they made the patient feel heard, which encouraged him to cooperate. I wish we had known years ago how effective these skills could be!

When you use the Yellow GPS skills at work to allow others to choose how to react and to assume more responsibility, you are demonstrating leadership and the art of delegation. Your job is not only something you do for a certain number of hours a week, it is also a showcase where you shine, where you are a role model, a mentor, and an inspiration to those around you. When you demonstrate to them how they are capable of doing more than they have been doing, it will enhance their lives and benefit your business. The following suggestions will help you streamline these strategies so that you can easily implement them in your work environment.

SUPPORT THE COLLECTIVE DECISION-MAKING PROCESS

DESCRIBE THE SITUATION

We just received a large order from a new client. In order to send them what they need on time, all of us will have to work much harder the next two weeks even though it is a holiday season and you are all overwhelmed as is. If we disappoint them we might lose them as a client, which will effect your end-of-year bonuses.

Here you share with your employees a behind the scenes view of what is going on instead of just letting them know about their extended work hours.

SHARE A LIFE LESSON

Despite the fact that this is the hectic holiday season, our major clients expect the same level of individual attention and willingness to go above and beyond. Sometimes, overlooking one small detail, despite legitimate reasons, can cause a client to go elsewhere. On the other hand, superb customer service, especially in a world as automated as ours is will always be appreciated and create unwavering loyalty.

Many times lucrative deals are sealed when a client receives superb customer service, despite their last-minute order. The client will remember this during the years they do business with you. Knowing this universal fact, that positive results and stellar customer service create repeat customers, will serve your employees and co-workers well. This knowledge, this life lesson, will make their investment and contribution in the company take on greater meaning.

GIVE A CHOICE

I want each of you to think about which days are easier for you to stay later. I welcome any other creative suggestions as to how we can make clients happier during this stressful season.

In the above example, you are demonstrating leadership by expecting everyone to be on board. You are leaving the

when and **how** up to your employees' discretion, but not the **if.** By doing this you are giving them a sense of control and are inviting their input on how to make things better. Does this mean that you and your co-workers will always be happy with the results of delegation and collaborative decision-making? Not necessarily. But had you unilaterally decided who does what and when, they might have felt resentful and unmotivated. Keep in mind it is never wise to offer choices if you aren't okay with all of the options. You can prevent this by giving them a list of choices, all of which are acceptable to you.

If you want to take this one step further, decide if there are times you can allow your employees to learn from their experience, even if they might make an unwise choice. Allowing this leeway and accepting less than excellent results might take you out of your comfort zone, so think this through before allowing it to happen. Below is an example of allowing an employee to make a decision that resulted in an unexpected outcome.

Sheila, a mother of three and a sought-after expert on international tax laws, shared this:

> *I was excited to implement the GPS skills at work. I had delegated the ordering of office and break-room supplies to a new employee and allowed her to decide if we should order from our usual supplier or go with a new start-up firm and save a significant amount.*
> *I was conducting an important meeting with out-of-town clients in the conference room. When she brought in the coffee I was mortified to see that there were no*

matching cups, no herbal tea, and not enough napkins. Later she explained to me that the previous suppliers had always delivered on time so we never ran out of supplies. The new company only delivered to our city once a week and she hadn't realized we were running short.

Sheila was very upset that the refreshments hadn't reflected her usual impeccable level of service. She was not okay with the repercussions of her employee's decision. This is an example of an unexpected disappointment.

It is your responsibility when deciding to let others take the lead to make sure you are comfortable with any possible outcomes which may result. The objective is to instill confidence in those around you, not set them up for failure.

Once you have clarified the Red Rules of your workplace, you can then move on to transferring Red/no situations to Yellow/trust ones. After proving themselves capable of following the rules, it is time to encourage your employees to participate in more challenging situations. By allowing others to take on more responsibility, you will not only free your time so it can be spent more productively, but you will become a role model they will want to emulate.

APPLYING THE SLIPPERY WHEN WET SIGN AT WORK

The Yellow road sign Slippery When Wet in the GPS skill set alerts us that caution is necessary. It is then up to you, the driver, to decide how to be careful in order to prevent dangerous accidents. How can you best use these Yellow skills to enhance your work experience?

Juggling a family, a home, and a career is extremely exhausting. You are constantly on the run and no matter how many things you accomplish in a day, you will always have a long to-do list still waiting for your attention. You want your children to be happy and your career to be successful. That means you are tired. Very tired!

Part of utilizing the Yellow Slippery When Wet skill set is to be aware of what you need to be able to function as well as possible under any circumstances. I am sure you haven't spent much time lately thinking about what you need, but in the spirit of this Yellow sign, take a few moments for introspection and contemplation. What do you need to be able to invest in your career while raising happy children?

Karen, a mother of two and a preschool director, had this to say:

I am up at 5:00 am because I need everything, including dinner, to be organized before I leave for the day. I am surrounded by children twenty-four seven because our school opens at 7:00 am to accommodate working moms. By the afternoon I am running on empty, so when I get home there is not much patience leftover for my daughters.

When we discussed this Yellow road sign in the group, I realized it was time I focused on myself. At first I felt guilty signing up for a Pilates group and reserving a weekly manicure slot. But when I saw how much I enjoyed the manicures and how energized I was after exercising, I was convinced that my children also benefitted from my new "mommy first" agenda.

What do you need to be able to invest in your career while raising happy children? You might prefer a weekly date with your partner or a monthly book club with a group of friends. Some career women find it empowering and rejuvenating to attend conferences and retreats connected to their profession. This allows them to combine education and time away meaningfully. Whatever it is you need, make it your priority. When you do, you will better be able to navigate the slippery slopes of business and career while raising a family.

DELAY YOUR INSTINCTIVE REACTION

Just like you automatically slow down when road conditions are dangerous, an effective Yellow GPS tactic is to intentionally be slow to respond. When tempers flare or when those around you are under pressure, sharing your opinion and reacting in the heat of the moment is usually detrimental. By recognizing the benefits of delaying your instinctive reaction, you will be empowering yourself to set an example during volatile situations.

> Employee: *I won't stand for having to put up with all these demands from clients. I know you say that the customer is always right, but this time I am right. I don't think I can continue working here anymore.*

Instead of an immediate response of, "If you feel that way, then there is the door" (which would leave you with one less employee) or due to the pressure give up your stellar customer service and say, "Ok, tell them they can't get the refund we promised," you can act responsibly and slow down your response.

> You: *I realize you are very upset now and understand there is good reason for that. Let's discuss this further, after the weekend, so we can come up with a plan that works for all of us.*

By not responding emotionally, by retaining control in the face of "slippery work conditions," you probably saved this person their job and prevented unnecessary inconvenience to your business and your clients.

APPLYING THE INTERSECTION AHEAD SIGN AT WORK

This Yellow road sign alerts us to changes ahead. Although most of the time your work is stable and repetitious, there are times when you know beforehand about changes which will need to be dealt with. Preparing yourself and those you work with, for these situations will create trust and stability.

Progress creates success, but it also means movement. In our constantly changing society we need to be intuitive to the needs of the industry and proactive when planning our professional future. Below are some ways the GPS Yellow skill set can help you achieve this.

GARNERING SUPPORT FOR WHAT LIES AHEAD

When those around you aren't prepared for the changes you are planning, you will have much less understanding, cooperation, and support from them. Why do many bosses, department heads, employees, and colleagues decide not to share information about impending developments?

Think about it. If you are planning to change jobs you don't want anyone to know about your plans. If you are contemplating a merger or planning to sell the company, your employees might find other employment options before the deal goes through. There are many logical reasons, some of them binding, not to share your work decisions with others.

But when you need the cooperation and support of those around you, you will be better off preparing them ahead of time. For example:

> *I told my supervisor I was planning to take a year off after my baby was born. At first, she was shocked and upset. After a few days she approached me with an offer to work two days a week from home. I hadn't even thought of this as an option. I am glad I had the courage to share my plans with her. This outcome is better than I had ever hoped for.*

By sharing what you are considering with those who will be impacted by your decisions, they will feel respected and connected. Not always will their reactions be what you hoped for, but as in the case above, sometimes you might be pleasantly surprised. Here is another example:

> *I invited the entire staff to a restaurant to thank them for making our company so successful and to personally prepare them for the upcoming merger. I found myself being asked details of what exactly would happen, but more importantly what wouldn't be happening. They were very relieved I had insisted on no staff changes for the first twelve months. It wasn't easy to achieve, but I felt that I owed them at least this much after all their years of devoted work.*

It is just as important to apprise others of what won't be happening, as well as what the impending changes will be.

Many times we overlook this vital component and thereby unwittingly create confusion or resistance because of the missing information. Being clear about what will and will not happen, will help you with your boss, your clients, and your co-workers and will create an atmosphere of trust which is necessary for long term success. Take a look at the example below:

> *Due to the economy we knew we would need to raise our prices at the beginning of the year. After reading about the GPS Yellow rules, I suggested we send emails to our long-time clients letting them know about this impending rise in costs and offering them a special deal if they prepaid for their upcoming year orders before the end of December. It was wildly successful because they felt valued as loyal clients and had the choice of taking advantage of the lower prices. We actually experienced the magic that happens when preparing others for impending changes.*

Despite all your good intentions, even if you let everyone impacted know about the changes ahead of time, always remember that it is you who has had the time and luxury to think about what you will be doing. If you elected to leave your job or close your business, you obviously have considered these options for quite a while.

Your employees, manager, clients, and work mates didn't know you were contemplating this decision and may be very upset by how it will impact their lives. This doesn't mean you need to remain stuck in a position which you feel you have outgrown. It does mean you need to prepare yourself for the fact that it will most likely be difficult for those around you to support or encourage you at such times.

This Yellow road sign symbolizes the importance of preparing others; it also symbolizes preparing yourself for negative feedback when you share your plans. Give those who are surprised by your information time and listen to their fears and concerns. Take their complaints seriously and if there is anything you can do to alleviate the difficulty, realize the importance of going that extra mile. People feel heard when you demonstrate compassion and good will and they then have an easier time moving forward, even if it wasn't what they would have chosen for themselves.

EMPOWERING OTHERS BY ENCOURAGING THEIR INPUT

Sudden changes make us feel out of control. When you invite people to be part of the solutions they feel empowered. Let's see how this can help you in the workplace. In most situations your employees, co-workers, and colleagues will have little say about what you are planning to do. But you can invite their input in various ways to make this upcoming change less disruptive for them.

Emily, a mother of five boys under the age of ten and a long-time dispatcher for her local police station, shared this example.

> *After a new police commissioner took over we knew there would be changes. We were very concerned. Most of the conversation during that time was*

275

worrying about the unknown. Imagine our surprise and delight when the new commissioner initiated a serious meet and greet. Everyone was in uniform and it was a bit intimidating, but the new commissioner insisted he wouldn't leave until each of us handed in some suggestions on how to improve our department. Because they used pen and paper and therefore suggestions were anonymous, we were able to make outrageous suggestions without fear of repercussion. Many of our ideas were implemented within the first year.

I have to admit that despite my misgivings, I enjoy work now more than ever. He doesn't realize it, but the commissioner used the Yellow skill set to prepare us when he insisted we participate in suggesting solutions and improvements. This made the transition easier on all of us.

Suggestions don't have to be offered anonymously. Most times people will be happy to share their concerns and insights. Even if you know you won't be able to implement all their proposals, make an effort to hear them out and show compassion for their struggles.

Using the Yellow GPS skills at work will create a safe zone for a more considered reaction and will encourage and allow your co-workers to do the same. Practice and implement these road rules and watch your career take off.

PART IV

PARTING WORDS TO KEEP YOU SAFELY ON THE ROAD

WHEN YOU'RE STUCK IN TRAFFIC

Do you sometimes feel that no matter what you say, what you do, what you try to modify and change, that you are still stuck in traffic? That despite all the newfound knowledge of how to use the road signs and traffic light signals as guidelines to better parenting methods, you are still stuck in a negative cycle with a child or a co-worker?

Despite having the latest model vehicle, even fully loaded, as well as the most updated GPS instructions, we can sometimes sit in traffic for hours, hardly inching forward. You might know precisely where you are going and exactly how to get there, but sometimes things beyond our control keep us stuck on the road.

Parenting is no different. The journey to successful joyous parenting can and does have bumps in the road. That doesn't mean you aren't on the right track. It does indicate that you would be wise to contemplate a slight change of course.

You have gone through the GPS program and now understand, have internalized, and are ready to implement many of the effective proven parenting methods. I am sure you have seen some, if not much, improvement both at home and at work. You have earned this wonderful sense of accomplishment through your dedication and perseverance.

But what happens when you just can't seem to get it right with a certain child or find a specific situation difficult with all of your children? What can you do when despite all the wisdom, clear instructions, real-life examples, and dialogues in this book, you can't seem to achieve the parenting goals you have set for yourself with your children? Or perhaps only one of your children is responding well to this new parenting method and the others are not? This can be even more annoying when you have proof it can work, but somehow for the others it doesn't. You feel frustrated, helpless, and stuck. What options are there in situations like these? What can you do about it?

FOCUS ON WHAT IS WORKING

The first thing to ask is, "What *is* working?" This might seem unnecessary to mention, but I find most of us tend to underestimate our achievements when we are faced with a problem or issue that stubbornly refuses to be fully resolved, despite all attempts on our part. We often lose sight of the overall improvement and minimize what we have been able to accomplish with that child or situation. The following is an example of this very common occurrence.

Brianna, a mother of three in her second marriage and a celebrated author, had this to say:

> I saw amazing improvement with my two oldest children since I started using the GPS skills with them. But no matter what I tried, I was still constantly in a power struggle with my four-year-old. I felt frustrated,

angry and to be perfectly honest, defeated. When I brought this up at a group meeting I was told to first analyze anything and everything that might have improved. After spending a few minutes comparing my current situation to how things were last year, I realized the tantrums and fighting didn't happen as often. I also noticed that although dinners and snacks used to be a huge issue, without me realizing it, we hardly argued about that anymore. Just recognizing these small improvements gave me the encouragement and motivation necessary to continue doing what was obviously working.

Zoey, a mother of two and the president of a rural hospital, shared the following:

I was thrilled to implement all of the GPS skill sets. They made so much sense and were easy to apply. My son responded immediately and our time together, although very limited due to my work schedule, was full of fun and love. My daughter was another story altogether. She stubbornly resisted every effort on my part to make things better. When I was advised to examine what was working, I noticed the only times I felt we were getting along were when I was alone with her. I realized when she was with her brother she was so busy trying to outdo him and get all my attention, that we were going around in circles. By realizing when things worked, I was able to set aside more alone time with her. By the end of the year our relationship was better than it had ever been!

What can we learn when analyzing these two very common situations? First, we tend to overlook small improvements and doom ourselves to being stuck in traffic, despite the fact that we are inching forward, albeit slowly. In addition, when we search for what is working, we might realize what allows that to happen. Zoey realized that her daughter responded much better when she wasn't competing with her brother for attention. Being aware of these important factors helps us realize that we aren't as stuck as we thought we were and can give us the missing insight or direction needed to be able to move forward, despite the disappointing results.

PARENT WITH GREEN, RED AND YELLOW

Another issue to be aware of is that in most situations, you as the parent can and should decide which of the different skills you want to use and why. By now you are proficient in using the GPS skills in all the colors and you know that successful parenting is a result of knowing how to use your authority, how to earn your child's trust, and how to express love and encouragement when dealing with most parenting dilemmas.

The following is a good example of how you can use your Red, Yellow and Green skills to respond to everyday situations.

Madison was at home sick and was very upset that her mother, Robin, was at work. She wasn't cooperating with her babysitter and kept calling her mother complaining. Before becoming familiar with the GPS system Robin would try to explain, then apologize, and then bribe Madison with something that she wanted. And finally, when all of these options didn't work, she would explode, insult Madison and ruin her day at work. When she got home she would often be resentful and exhausted and usually would end the day feeling like the worst mother ever.

After gaining the necessary insight as to why she found it so difficult to assert herself with Madison while at work, and by using the GPS skills, Robin was able to respond to Madison in a confident manner which enabled her to enjoy coming home after a successful day in her store. This is how she did it. After assessing the situation, she decided to use a combination of all three parenting components. Robin used the Red/No skills by asserting her authority and teaching a life lesson.

Madison, when I am at work, you are not to call me unless there is an emergency. Having a cold doesn't constitute an emergency. Ella, the babysitter, will decide when something is urgent and when I need to be called.

Robin used her authority to decide who she would accept calls from and under what circumstances. By doing so, she also taught Madison a life lesson about the importance of respecting other people's time. This life lesson will serve Madison well in the coming years. She then added the Yellow/Slow skills, giving Madison choices and trusting her to choose one that would be good for her.

> *Until I come home, you can read, use your sticker book, or rest. If you want to speak to somebody, here is Grandma's cell phone number. She said she would be delighted to hear from you. I trust you to decide how you want to spend your time until I come home.*

Robin allowed Madison to feel in control by giving her enjoyable options. By encouraging Madison to decide how she wanted to spend her sick day, Robin gave her a vote of confidence, which positively affected Madison's self-image and put her in a good mood. Robin then elected to add the Green/Go skill by committing to spending quality time with Madison later in the evening after she arrived home.

> *While I am at work, why don't you think of something special we can do later tonight? I will be thinking about you during work today and when we snuggle, play a game, or read a story tonight I will be able to show you how much I love you, even though I can't be home during the day.*

Now Madison is assured that she is loved and important, despite the many hours her mother spends at work and even on a day that she is home not feeling well.

As a result of using the effective GPS skills, Robin arrives home after a successful day at work with minimum interruptions and much less guilt. She can even express pride in Madison's considerate behavior and look forward to spending time with her that evening.

The next time you feel stuck, either with a specific child or in a certain situation, ask yourself if you are accessing the wide array of skills you now possess. Maybe you are using only one kind of skill because you feel most comfortable with that one or because it has always been effective until now. This might be when you need to combine more than one GPS skill set to achieve the result you want. Sometimes it is precisely these difficult situations that force us to move out of our comfort zones and explore capabilities we didn't know we possessed. So be brave enough to try something new and see how your child flourishes as a result.

REMEMBER THAT ALL CHILDREN ARE DIFFERENT

This goes without saying. You know that each of your children was born on a different date, has their own set of fingerprints, and their own unique characteristics. Yet despite this common knowledge, when starting a new parenting method and hoping for positive results, we often overlook this undisputed fact.

Before you decide that nothing is working with a particular child, ask yourself if you are expecting the same or similar results from all of your children. If you are, then my best advice would be to remind yourself that although all your children have much in common and are being raised by you in the same house, each is a unique individual. It might simply be that this child is a slow-moving vehicle compared to your other children. Or maybe this child needs a different environment in which to be able to shine. Yes, each child has his or her own challenges, their own life script to figure out and their own individual future success story.

Never lose sight of the fact that each of them marches to a different drummer. Use your creativity, perseverance, and the entire menu of GPS skills to create the right roadmap for each of your children. You were given these children as gifts to love, guide, and treasure. You are capable of succeeding!

RECALCULATE WHEN NECESSARY

Remember what a GPS says when you miss your exit or there is a detour on the road? It says "recalculating" while it figures out an alternate route for you to take. Even if you are facing "inclement weather" or a "blocked road" in your parenting journey, don't give up. Don't remain stuck in traffic. Instead, recalculate and find another way.

Realize that there isn't something wrong with you, your child, or with the system. It may be that what worked for the others isn't working as well for this child. That's part of life. The important thing is not to turn off the ignition and stay stuck on the road forever. This is the time to use all your knowledge and experience in trying to find the reason for being blocked and more importantly, another way to tackle the issue. It is precisely situations like these for which the book you are reading has a built-in re-calculator. Use it when necessary and you will reach your destination.

SEEK PROFESSIONAL GUIDANCE IF NEEDED

Take into consideration that your child may have learning disabilities or social issues which haven't been discovered and may need professional evaluation. This may be slowing down his or her progress when compared to what you are experiencing with your other children. When despite all your efforts, you still see no improvement, it's time to move on to something different.

If despite everything you have read, learned, internalized, and implemented, and you still feel that the situation is not improving, this might be a good time to seek professional help. There are many qualified people who can be of help in these situations. Maybe you are currently in an emotional state that is making it more difficult for you to parent with confidence. Discussing things with a professional might give you the clarity, insight, and direction you are missing. You might benefit from the one-on-one focus of a phone coaching session on parenting or you might be in need of more personal insight and deeper, more intense work. Gift yourself the experience of sharing your challenges with someone who can enlighten and empower you. It will change your life.

A WORKING MOTHER'S FINAL Q&A AND GPS WRAP-UP

I notice I choose only certain skills to use. Why is that?

I mentioned earlier that many mothers find they gravitate toward using only certain skills from the many suggested in the program. This sometimes creates situations in which they feel stuck in traffic. When discussing this phenomenon with working mothers I noticed that if left unchecked, invariably they will choose to use the skills which resonate most with their personalities and values. This means that a mother who feels more comfortable being assertive will automatically use the Red skills when dealing with her children as opposed to a mother who highly values independence and collaboration and might choose the Green or Yellow skills as her first choice.

There is nothing wrong with feeling more comfortable using certain skills. But the focus of this parenting system is on what our child needs from us at any given time. If you notice that things aren't moving along at the pace you had anticipated, see what happens if you go out of your comfort zone and try to implement some of the other skills you haven't used regularly. This might be exactly what your child is missing. Even if not, you will have demonstrated more balance and creativity in your parenting. Balance and creativity are always a win.

How do I notice small changes in my children and at work?

A good way to notice change is to ask yourself if you see any difference in the following three areas; duration, frequency, and intensity. This means that when you are searching for progress in any area, if you see there is a difference in any of these three categories you can rest assured that you are on the right track. If your toddler's tantrums have been less frequent, less intense, or maybe last for a shorter amount of time, you should continue what you are doing because it is working. If your critical or aggressive boss's tirades have been less frequent, less intense, or don't last quite as long as they used to, then you are on the right track. Being aware of these different parameters of change, you might realize that although you feel as though you are stuck, transformation, however slight, has begun to take place. Rejoice and continue being the wonderful working mother you are.

How do I know when to seek outside help?

An important parenting rule, and life lesson, is not to give up prematurely. Children are our pride, our future, and our legacy. Many times, they are also our greatest challenge. By dealing with the difficulties our children create, we are compelled to rise above our current capabilities and grow. Before you seek professional advice, ask yourself which suggestions mentioned in the GPS skill sets you have not tried yet and what you can do differently. Then give yourself the necessary time to see if what you are attempting to change is taking hold.

Notice any progress, no matter how minor. Only after you are sure that you have exhausted all of the GPS skill sets, should you consider an evaluation for your child or for yourself as a parent. Of course, if a nanny or teacher points out academic, social or other types of limitations, reach out for professional help immediately. Time is of the essence, especially during the early years that are so vital to your child's development.

Some mothers prefer gifting themselves with the service of a personal coach while navigating the many road signs of the GPS system. If you can commit to this option, it might help you feel more empowered while going through the program. If this is not possible for you right now, it might be a better choice for you to invest in my online program, which will allow you to practice the many GPS skills using the powerful exercises and resources, at your convenience. By immersing yourself in this life-changing program, you will gain the confidence and competence to deal with the inevitable challenges of raising children while investing in your career. Whatever you decide, remember that you are in the driver's seat and as long as you know what your destination is, with perseverance, dedication, and by making wise choices, you will get there.

ON A PERSONAL NOTE

Do you remember the night I decided that I needed to find a better way to raise my children while working full time? When I needed to remove my four-year old son from his stakeout in front of the door so I could give a lecture to other mothers on how to successfully combine mothering with work? I think back and ask myself, "Had I created the Working Mother's GPS before that evening, what could I have done differently that night? What other options would I have been able to choose from had I known then what I now know?"

Had I known about the many GPS skills I would have used the Yellow skills to prepare him in advance for me having to leave that evening. We could have brainstormed together beforehand to discover what we could do to make it easier for him to say goodbye calmly when the time came for me to leave. Had we both been prepared, it wouldn't have been so traumatic. I would have invited him to be part of the solution and most likely used the language of responsibility to gently remind him what we had discussed and what he had agreed to do. I would also have had a wide array of Red skills to choose from. I could have chosen a family Red Rule, which would pertain to my necessary evening work out of the home. I would have brought up the reasons he may resist (you wish mommy didn't have to leave now), been his lawyer (I know the reason you want me to stay home is because you want us to have a good time together, not because you want to make me miss my lecture) and would have given him information (mommy is running late so I need to leave right now) instead of saying, "No I can't stay home another minute." It also would have been very helpful if at that time I had understood how to prevent situations from escalating and how to respond without reacting.

Had I chosen to use the Green skills, I would have made sure to express my love and appreciation and used a compliment when catching him doing something good. I would have also created an important routine or tradition for the evenings when I needed to leave. This would have gone a long way in helping us calmly deal with needing to say goodbye. I would also have been aware of the necessity and option to find creative solutions if this situation had repeated itself time and again.

This is just a partial list of the many choices which would have been available to me had I created this parenting program before that fateful evening. I would have been able to deal with the nerve-wracking situation with clarity and confidence while asserting my authority, earning his trust, and creating a strong loving connection despite the need for me to go to work. I know I would have been able to give the lecture that evening feeling much less guilty, knowing that my parenting skills allowed me to invest in my career while raising children who felt loved and understood.

You are about to finish reading this book. You have heard many working mothers just like you sharing their personal stories of trial and error, of challenge and change. You have discovered how the universal road signs, so much an integral part of our lives, symbolize the three vital components necessary in successful parenting, love, authority and trust.

You have reviewed the prevalent bumps in the road and have read about many effective tactics to speed up the process. The answers to questions many mothers ask have informed and enlightened you and the examples on how to apply this method at work have hopefully empowered you.

The rest is up to you. You now have the knowledge and the skills. Ahead of you is the road to successful, powerful, and practical parenting. You know what you want to accomplish and now you know the best way to achieve those goals.

I will leave you with the two questions I always hear at the end of my parenting course.

Should I begin implementing this method if my partner is not on board?

There is no question that it is much easier, more effective and actually much more fun when parents or partners are raising children with the same values, methods, and proven techniques. It makes things clearer for everyone involved and creates a consistently stable home, which is optimal. But not every family situation is so simple.

You may be a single mom raising your children alone or you might be dealing with the challenges of a blended family. In my online GPS program you will find a special resource focused on how to use the GPS skills pertaining to your specific family situation. You might be in a marriage where your husband has little interest in joining you in implementing this proven parenting program or maybe you are out of the house so much that most of your children's waking hours are spent with paid caretakers. Whatever your reality might be, always remember that you are in the driver's seat. Because you are their mother, you have a tremendous amount of influence on the kind of relationship you will have with your children.

Despite the possible lack of cooperation or support, know that every time you exert your authority, each time you earn your child's trust, every loving word you express is valuable and indelible. Your children will perceive you as a loving, responsible, and accessible parent who knows what she is doing and why. Instead of waiting for the understanding and support you so legitimately yearn for, begin implementing the vast menu of skills in which you have gained proficiency through studying this program. Even if you are alone parenting this way, your children will gain immeasurably.

Should I put off implementing this parenting program until my schedule is less hectic and I have the time to invest in this life-changing program?

I will answer this question by sharing a personal story that has greatly affected my life ever since it happened almost four decades ago.

I was living far away from my family and friends and was a mother of a beautiful eighteen-month-old daughter. We were living very frugally because I was paying for my academic studies while trying to save to open a private practice after completing my internship. I hardly bought anything that wasn't necessary, which precluded me from purchasing expensive clothing for my adorable daughter.

One day I received a love package from my mother who lived thousands of miles away. My daughter was her oldest granddaughter and she had invested in a beautiful expensive dress knowing that at that time I didn't have the means to do so myself. The minute the package arrived I unwrapped the box. Opening it I caught my breath. Inside was the most gorgeous toddler's dress I had ever seen, adorned by sparkles, tulle, smocking, and ribbons. To me it looked like something out of a fairytale.

Even at her young age my daughter realized this was a very special occasion. She stood perfectly still as I zipped her up and took her to see herself in the mirror. Compared to her usual outfits, this dress created a magical transformation; my little one looked like a royal princess and my heart burst with joy. As I stood admiring her, I realized that an ordinary Monday afternoon was no time for her to wear this magnificent dress. I explained this to her as I reverently took the dress off and wrapped it in the tissue paper that had kept it pristine as it crossed oceans to reach our humble home and put it carefully back in the box.

During the following weeks, I was on the lookout for an opportunity to dress her in that beautiful dress. It wasn't appropriate to wear to the grocery or the playground and it definitely wasn't made for lazy mornings playing with toys at home. We didn't have parties to attend and we weren't invited to any weddings. Weeks and months flew by without my finding the right time to use the dress.

One day I realized that I had not sent my mother a photograph of her first granddaughter dressed in the beautiful outfit she had sent. I decided to dress up my princess in the magical dress and take as many photos as possible before she tired of cooperating. My mother had inquired countless times about the dress and I wanted to send her a photo album of her most adorable granddaughter so she could share the photos with her friends and neighbors.

Imagine my disbelief and horror when I tried dressing my daughter and realized that the dress was much too small! No amount of pushing, pulling, or praying would get that tiny zipper to close. I was devastated. I am not ashamed to admit that I cried copious tears over what others would describe as an unimportant incident. But for me it was beyond painful. It was proof that by waiting for the perfect moment I had lost all the moments she could have enjoyed the dress. It became the first and last dress that she never wore.

From that day forward I was determined to make the most of every opportunity. By waiting for the perfect moment, I had lost too much. Whenever I had the opportunity to have fun with my children, I did so. I no longer waited until the house was clean, the homework was done, or my reports for work were filed. Seizing the moment, I sang, danced, baked, and had picnics under the dining-room table on rainy days, making the most of every moment. The beautiful dress had taught me all I ever wanted to know about "waiting for the perfect moment." I had learned that life passes you by while you wait for perfect moments to happen.

Since then, every time I think it will be best to postpone something important for a better time, a calmer time, a more conducive time, I remember that beautiful never-worn dress wrapped in yellowing tissue paper. And miraculously the perfectly imperfect moment becomes that very minute.

Remember the message of that never-worn dress. Realize the perfect time for anything that is important to you is now. If you wait until your life isn't as hectic or until you aren't busy with a thousand other important things, you might find your children have grown up and left home and you will have missed the opportunity to raise them with confidence and joy using this unique parenting program. Grab this opportunity to begin implementing the many GPS skills you have discovered in this book, and despite the many hours you spend at work, enjoy raising your children while they are still young. Use this powerful, practical and proven parenting program and see how it can change your life from this very moment forward. The perfect time to start down the road to your parenting success is now.

THE WORKING MOTHER'S ONLINE GPS PROGRAMS

I f you loved what you just read in my book, *A Working Mother's GPS: A Guide to Parenting Success,* and want to deepen your understanding of the Green, Red, and Yellow Light Parenting System to gain greater success at home and at work, register online at www.AtaraMalach.com for one of my programs.

1. Guidelines to Parenting Success (GPS) Online Self-Study Program

- ➢ Lifetime access to this groundbreaking online parenting program.
- ➢ Five modules, including twenty-six short powerful and practical lessons.
- ➢ Exclusive "Parenting Color Interactive Quiz."
- ➢ Fifty empowering exercises to help you define and design your Parenting Roadmap.
- ➢ Twenty important resource materials.
- ➢ Bonus mini-course on work/life balance.

2. Guidelines to Professional Success (GPS) Online Self-Study Program

- ➢ Lifetime access to this career-focused online program about the practical application of the GPS skills in your workplace.

➢ Ten lessons and twenty exercises to guide you through creating your personalized Career Roadmap.
➢ Six valuable resource materials.
➢ Bonus discount for a mini-course on time management.

3. Three-Month Mastermind Group Coaching GPS Program

➢ All benefits of the GPS parenting program described above.
➢ Weekly group coaching calls with other working mothers and the program creator and parenting expert, Atara Malach.

4. VIP One-Day Intensive GPS Immersion Online Program

➢ Lifetime access to both GPS Programs outlined above, including all accompanying materials.
➢ Two three-hour virtual sessions via video conferencing with GPS creator and parenting expert, Atara Malach.
➢ Personalized support in applying both the Parenting Roadmap and the Career Roadmap to your specific circumstances and desires.
➢ Follow-up implementation strategy call with Atara within thirty days of completing this VIP Immersion Day.

5. Total Results Exclusive VIP GPS Personal Coaching Six-Month Program

This exclusive program is reserved solely for the most discerning and highly invested clients who desire the utmost in personal attention and discretion. In addition to all benefits of the four programs listed above, this program offers:

> ➤ Nine hours over six months of confidential and individualized power coaching calls with parenting expert, Atara Malach.
>
> ➤ Atara's highly attentive one-on-one guidance and full customization of both GPS programs for the greatest impact on your home life and career.
>
> ➤ Email access to Atara through your private client portal for questions and concerns between coaching calls.
>
> ➤ Follow-up "Total Results" call within thirty days of completing this program.

Personal, powerful coaching with Atara Malach: Information on coaching packages designed to help you create the life you have always dreamed of can be found at AtaraMalach.com

Information about the GPS online programs can be found on my website AtaraMalach.com To share your experiences raising happy children you can email me at atara@ataramalach.com

ABOUT THE AUTHOR

As a young mother working to establish her own counseling practice, Atara Malach knew firsthand the demands and stresses of a woman stretched to her physical, mental, and emotional limits. Her instincts told her there had to be a better way.

Atara established her private practice in 1987 and has dedicated the past thirty years of her life helping tens of thousands of people across the globe achieve their professional and personal goals. After parenting her own children, one of Atara's greatest joys is connecting with working mothers and guiding them along the many different stages of their work/life journey.

During her years in private practice and while using her passion for helping working mothers, Atara has developed a proven parenting system that gives her clients the tools and confidence to manage their many priorities and find calm in the chaos of their daily demands. In her practice and personal coaching sessions, with her own family, and with thousands of professional women and working parents, Atara has tested and refined her GPS Parenting System. She now presents her program in her new book, *A Working Mother's GPS: A Guide to Parenting Success for the Modern Working Mom.*

She has also developed a *Premier Individual VIP Coaching Program* for discerning clients, such as career-minded mothers, executives, and business owners. This VIP coaching program is focused on clients who choose to invest more deeply, in order to achieve exponential success in their businesses and their personal lives.

Atara founded a parenting academy at the beginning of her professional career and created a curriculum for the more than 600 families who participated in weekly classes. This new book, *A Working Mother's GPS: A Guide to Parenting Success for The Modern Working Mom,* is the culmination of these decades of experience.

Atara has enjoyed the immense privilege of sharing this system worldwide through exclusive one-on-one coaching relationships, workshops, online programs, and lectures. Atara has conducted hundreds of presentations and workshops that were presented to global audiences. In these experiences she has focused on helping her many diverse clients create and enjoy a healthy work/life balance by enhancing their inherent strengths and guiding them in how to create an environment, with their children and in their career, that is conducive to their personal and professional growth.

Atara's methods are easily applicable and consist of providing clear actionable solutions which create the desired results. Through exclusive personal coaching, products and online programs, she shares her proven systems and strategies to enhance career development and help women be amazing mothers, while at the same time leveraging their professional skills to enhance their professional relationships.

Atara has focused on, and invested in, becoming an expert on career and personal development, relationship management, and conflict resolution. *A Working Mother's GPS: A Guide to Parenting Success for The Modern Working Mom*, based on Atara's innovative parenting method, will educate and give inspiration to the many mothers struggling with work/life balance. This is the first time the general public will have access to this unique groundbreaking parenting program.

For more about Atara see her LinkedIn profile: https://www.linkedin.com/in/ataramalach

Atara's new online parenting program, *GPS for the Working Mom*, is available on her website at www.AtaraMalach.com

CPSIA information can be obtained
at www.ICGtesting.com
Printed in the USA
LVHW081601080319
609995LV00016B/719/P

9 781948 787086